...when you need it in writing! ™

PERSONNEL MANAGER

More than 200 agreements, forms, letters, memos and documents to help you manage your personnel files effectively and legally.

LAWPACK™

First published 1997
Second edition 1999
Third edition 2002

Published by
Law Pack Publishing Limited
76-89 Alscot Road
London SE1 3AW

www.lawpack.co.uk

Copyright © 2002 Law Pack Publishing Ltd

ISBN 1 904053 23 8

IMPORTANT FACTS
ABOUT THIS LAW PACK BOOK

Law Pack publications are designed to provide authoritative and accurate information on the subject matter covered. However, neither this nor any other publication can take the place of a solicitor on important legal matters.

This **Law Pack** publication is sold on the understanding that the publisher, author and retailer are not engaged in rendering legal services. If legal advice or other expert assistance is required, the services of a competent professional should be sought.

The forms included in this **Law Pack** publication cover many everyday matters, but we cannot cater for all circumstances. If what you want is not included, we advise you to see a solicitor.

This **Law Pack** publication is designed only for use in England and Wales. It is not suitable for Scotland or Northern Ireland.

The information this book contains has been carefully compiled from reliable sources but its accuracy is not guaranteed as laws and regulations may change or be subject to differing interpretations.

As with any legal matter, common sense should determine whether you need the assistance of a solicitor rather than relying solely on the information and forms in this **Law Pack** book.

We strongly urge you to consult a solicitor whenever substantial amounts of money are involved, or where you do not understand the instructions or are uncertain how to complete and use a form correctly, or if you have any doubts about its adequacy to protect you, or if what you want to do is not precisely covered by the forms provided.

PRINTED IN GREAT BRITAIN
LAW PACK PUBLISHING LIMITED
76-89 ALSCOT ROAD LONDON SE1 3AW

About Personnel Manager...

Personnel Manager contains all the important and ready-to-complete forms and documents you need to manage your company's or organisation's employees.

Virtually every personnel record-keeping form is at your fingertips, giving you the protection you need without the inconvenience or cost of using a solicitor for simple personnel matters you can easily handle yourself.

Law Pack's *Personnel Manager* is the ideal way to 'get it in writing'. What better way to legally document your important personnel agreements and contracts, avoid troublesome disputes, enforce your legal rights, comply with legal obligations and avoid liability?

Virtually every size and type of organisation can use *Personnel Manager*. It can be used by both non-profit-making and profit-making businesses to document employee turnover, agreements, salaries and policies. It will be particularly useful to time-starved small and medium-sized businesses, which can easily keep up-to-date, accurate and valuable personnel records with this book.

How to Use Personnel Manager

Using **Law Pack's** *Personnel Manager* is easy by following these simple instructions.

1 To find the appropriate form, look through the two tables of contents. The first lists them by category in Sections; the second alphabetically. Consult Section Glossaries for summaries of each form.

2 You may find several forms for the same general purpose, read through and select the form most appropriate for your specific needs.

3 Cut out and photocopy the form you want and keep the original so it can be used again in the future. Alternatively you can use the form as a template to prepare your own documents. Letter-type documents can be personalised by being reproduced on your own letterhead.

4 Complete each form fully. Make certain all blanks (name, address, dates, amounts) are filled in. You may need to delete or add provisions in some forms to suit your requirements. If this is necessary, make sure each deletion or insertion is initialled by all parties. If there is not enough space on the document to make your insertion, it is best to type out the entire document, including the insertion, on a new sheet of paper.

5 Some forms and sections have noted instructions, which should be observed if you are to use the form or forms properly. Some forms refer to other forms in this Personnel Manager, other documents or copies of documents which will need to be attached to the form before use.

6 The pronoun 'it' within a form can refer to an individual as well as a business entity. The pronoun 'he' can refer to a woman as appropriate.

About Agreements

Under English law a contract does not have to be written down to be valid and enforceable. A verbal contract has just as much validity as a written contract. The problem associated with a verbal contract is that if there is a dispute over the contract the only evidence of the terms of the contract is the verbal evidence of each party to the contract which will be based on memory.

The reason that important contracts are written down, therefore, is so that a written record exists of what was agreed between the parties, to minimise the possibility of later disputes.

A contract exists where two or more parties make mutual promises to each other to take some sort of action or to make some payment to each other. An exchange of goods for money is the simplest form of contract. A simple promise by A to B, however, is not a contract, because B has given no 'consideration' to A's promise. In order to turn A's promise into an enforceable contract B must also make some promise or payment in return (the consideration). A contract like this involving mutual promises can be referred to as both a contract and an agreement, and both terms are used to mean the same thing in Personnel Manager.

Signature of Agreements: The part of an agreement that the parties sign is known as the attestation clause. In simple agreements, the attestation clause is the same for both companies and individuals. Each party should sign the agreement and also get a witness to sign and provide his or her name and address if indicated.

Use caution and common sense when using Personnel Manager– or any other do-it-yourself legal product. Whilst these forms are generally considered appropriate for self-use, you must nevertheless decide when you should seek professional legal advice instead. You should consult a solicitor if:

- You need a complex or important agreement.

- Your transaction involves substantial amounts of money or expensive property.

- You don't understand how to use a document – or question its adequacy to fully protect you.

Because we cannot be certain that the forms in this book are appropriate to your circumstances – or are being properly used – we cannot assume any liability or responsibility in connection with their use.

Table of Contents - By Category

Section 1 Recruiting & Hiring

Section 2 Employee Introduction & Management

New Employees

Personnel Management

Temporary Employees

Section 3 Employment Terms

Agreements & Procedures

Payroll

Working Hours

Section 4 Employment Benefits & Leave

Expenses & Benefits

Section 5 Performance Evaluation

Evaluation

Grievances

Section 6 Termination

Table of Contents - Alphabetical

Section 1
Recruiting & Hiring

Advertising & Applying:

Acknowledgement Letter to Applicant – Acknowledges applicant's response to advertisement for position.

Application Disclaimer and Acknowledgement – Affirms correctness of application and authorises release of information.

Applicant Waiver – Certifies the accuracy of an application and acknowledges no guarantee of employment.

Application for Employment – Detailed record of applicant's education employment history and skills.

Application for Employment: Preliminary – A summary of applicant's employment goals and history.

Available Position Notice – Lists duties and qualifications for employment opening.

Help Wanted Advertising Listing – Records information for placing an advertisement to fill a job opening.

Job Bid – Records current employee's interest in another position within company.

Interviewing & Confirming:

Appointment Rescheduled Letter – Notifies applicant of change in appointment date.

Comparison Summary of Applicants – Compares the job requirements ratings of three candidates.

Confirmation of Employment – Confirms acceptance of employment offer with successful candidate.

Interview Confirmation – Confirms date and time of applicant's scheduled interview.

Interview Schedule – Lists dates and times of interviews scheduled for various positions.

Interview Summary – Summarises an applicant's impressions on and responses to an interviewer's questions.

No Decision on Recruitment Letter – Letter informing applicant of company's indecision to fill position.

Notification to Applicant - Letter asking the applicant to telephone the employer to discuss the position available.

Rating of Applicant 1 – Rates an individual applicant on job requirements.

Rating of Applicant 2 – Rates an individual's education, experience, interpersonal and communication skills.

Rating of Applicant: Clerical – Rates an individual applicant's office skills.

Rejection Letter 1 – Letter rejecting an applicant.

Rejection Letter 2 – Letter rejecting an applicant.

Rejection Letter 3 – Letter rejecting an applicant.

Reply to Applicant – Negative response to applicant's inquiry regarding employment opportunities.

References & Checking up:

Authorisation to Release Information – Authorises the release of education and employment information.

Medical Records Request – Requests the release of medical information.

Medical Testing Authorisation – Grants authority to perform specific medical tests.

Reference Acknowledgement - Letter acknowledging receipt of reference from another company.

Reference by Telephone Record - Records information about employee references given by telephone.

Reference by Telephone Checklist – Records reference responses to questions regarding a specific applicant.

Reference Request by Applicant – A letter requesting an employment reference from a previous employer.

Reference Request by Employment – Requests employment information from previous employer.

Transcript Request – Requests a copy of examination certificates and attendance record.

Verification of Background – Verifies the educational and career background of an employee.

Verification of Education – Verifies an applicant's education record.

Verification of Employment – Verifies an applicant's employment record.

Verification of Qualification– Verifies an applicant's licence or registration.

ACKNOWLEDGEMENT LETTER TO APPLICANT

Date _____

To _____

_____

_____

Dear _____

Thank you for responding to our advertisement for the position of

_____

Your qualifications appear to meet the minimum requirements for the position. As scheduling permits, we would like to arrange for an interview at our offices located at

_____

Please call _____ at _____ to make an appointment for your interview.

Thank you for your interest in the above position.

Yours sincerely,

_____

Personnel Manager

APPLICATION DISCLAIMER
AND ACKNOWLEDGEMENT

To: _____

I certify that the information contained in this application is correct to the best of my knowledge. I understand that to falsify information is grounds for your refusing to engage or employ me, or for instant dismissal without notice or pay in lieu should I be employed.

I authorise any person, organisation or company listed on this application to provide you with any and all information concerning my previous employment, education and qualifications for employment. I also authorise you to request and receive such information.

_____   _____

Signature of applicant   Date

APPLICANT WAIVER
(All job applicants must sign and submit with application form)

To: _____

I hereby certify that the information contained in the attached application form is correct to the best of my knowledge and belief. I understand that falsification of this information is grounds for your refusing to engage or employ me or, if employed, instant dismissal, without notice or pay in lieu.

I hereby authorise any of the persons or organisations listed in my application to give all information concerning my previous employment, education, or any other information they might have, personal or otherwise, with regard to any of the subjects covered by this application, and I hereby release all such parties from all and any liability that may result from providing such information to you. I authorise you to request and receive such information.

I understand that no representative of the company has any authority to enter into any agreement for employment for any specified period of time, or assure or make some other personnel move, either prior to commencement of employment or after I have become employed, or to assure any benefits or terms and conditions of employment, or make any agreement contrary to the foregoing.

I hereby acknowledge that I have been advised that this application will remain under consideration for no more than 90 days from the date it was signed.

_____   _____
Applicant   Date

_____   _____
Company Representative   Date

APPLICATION FOR EMPLOYMENT
(please print)

Full Name: _____

Address: _____ Town: _____

Post code:_____ Country: _____ Tel: _____

Position applied for: _____

Are you a citizen of the EU or EEA?　　❑　Yes　　❑　No

If not, do you have a work permit?_____

EDUCATION

Secondary School with dates: _____

Exams passed with grades _____

_____

_____

College/Univ. with dates: _____

Degree:_____

Postgrad/Other qualifications with dates: _____

Degree: _____

PREVIOUS EMPLOYMENT
(begin with most recent position)

Most recent

Firm: _____ Address: _____

Supervisor: _____ Nature of business: _____

Dates of employment: _____ Position(s) held: _____

Ending salary: _____ Reason for leaving: _____

Previous Employer

Firm: _____ Address: _____

Supervisor: _____ Nature of business: _____

Dates of employment: _____ Position(s) held: _____

Ending salary: _____ Reason for leaving: _____

continued on next page

Previous Employer

Firm: _____ Address:_____

Supervisor:_____ Nature of Business: _____

Dates of employment: _____ Position(s) Held: _____

Ending Salary:_____ Reason for Leaving:_____

REFERENCES

Please provide the names and addresses of two people to whom you are not related and by whom you have not been employed.

Name:_____

Address: _____

Name:_____

Address: _____

Who referred you to us? (person or agency):_____

_____

Summarise your special skills or qualifications:

_____

_____

_____

I certify that my answers are true and complete to the best of my knowledge.

I authorise you to make such investigations and inquiries of my personal, employment, educational, financial, or medical history and other related matters as may be necessary for an employment decision. I hereby release employers, schools, or persons from all liability in responding to inquiries in connection with my application.

In the event that I am employed, I understand that false or misleading information given in my application or interview(s) may result in discharge.

Signature of Applicant:_____ Date: _____

For Department Use Only

Action: _____

_____

_____

APPLICATION FOR EMPLOYMENT: PRELIMINARY

I understand that this is not a full application. I understand this application will be reviewed and my qualifications considered for possible job openings in the future.

Name: _____ Date: _____

Address: _____ Town: _____

Post code: _____ Country: _____ Tel: _____

Position desired: _____ Requested salary: £ _____ per ____

TYPE OF EMPLOYMENT

☐ Seasonal ☐ Temporary ☐ Permanent ☐ Full-time ☐ Part-time

Days available: ☐ Monday to Friday ☐ Other (explain) _____

_____

_____. Hours available: _____ to ____

EMPLOYMENT

Most recent or previous employer: _____

Dates employed: _____ to: _____ Salary: £ _____ per _____

Describe position & duties: _____

EDUCATION

Enter the number of years completed:

Secondary school: _____ College/University: _____ Postgrad etc: _____

Describe your major areas of studies: _____

_____

Other training: _____

List other information for the employment you are seeking: _____

_____

All potential employees are evaluated without regard to race, colour, religion, gender, national origin, age, marital status or disability.

Signature: _____ Date: _____

Print Name: _____

AVAILABLE POSITION NOTICE

Starting date:_____ Date posted:_____

Position:_____

Description of duties:

_____

_____

_____

_____

_____

Qualifications required:

_____

_____

_____

_____

_____

_____

Salary _____

Contact _____

HELP WANTED ADVERTISING LISTING

Position: _____ Req. No: _____

Department/Division: _____

Charge to: _____
(Department)

Person requesting ad: _____ Phone Ext.: _____

Newspaper: _____

Run ad: _____ (days) _____
(dates)

Under classified heading: _____

Please insert the following ad:

For Department Use Only

Ad placed: _____ (date) _____
(newspaper)

Cost: £_____

Ad to run: _____ (days) _____
(dates)

Re-run ordered: _____ (date) _____
(newspaper)

Re-run cost: £_____

Responses:

_____

_____

_____

_____

JOB BID

Employee _____ Date_____

Current Department_____

Current Supervisor_____

Position applying for _____Dept _____

Qualifications for the job _____

_____

_____

_____

Other qualifications (degrees, etc.)_____

_____

_____

_____

_____

Employee signature

For Department use only

Date employee interviewed _____

Did employee get the job?   _____ Yes   _____ No

If not, why not?_____

_____

Has employee's supervisor been notified?_____

Has employee been notified?_____

_____

Department Representative

APPOINTMENT RESCHEDULED LETTER

Date _____

To _____

_____

_____

Dear _____

Your appointment with _____on _____
at _____m. has been rescheduled.

Please accept our apologies for any inconvenience this may cause you.

Your new appointment is scheduled for _____m. on_____

If you are unable to make this appointment, please call _____
at_____to re-schedule.

We look forward to meeting you then.

Yours sincerely,

_____

Personnel Manager

COMPARISON SUMMARY OF APPLICANTS

Position: _____ Date: _____

Interviewer:_____

Candidate A: _____

Candidate B: _____

Candidate C: _____

Legend:
1   Meets job requirements
2   Exceeds job requirements
0   Does not meet job requirements

Job Requirements	A	B	C	Comments
_____	_____	_____	_____	_____
_____	_____	_____	_____	_____
_____	_____	_____	_____	_____
_____	_____	_____	_____	_____
_____	_____	_____	_____	_____
_____	_____	_____	_____	_____
_____	_____	_____	_____	_____
_____	_____	_____	_____	_____
_____	_____	_____	_____	_____
_____	_____	_____	_____	_____
_____	_____	_____	_____	_____
_____	_____	_____	_____	_____
_____	_____	_____	_____	_____
_____	_____	_____	_____	_____

CONFIRMATION OF EMPLOYMENT

Date _____

To _____

_____

_____

Dear _____

Post of _____

Following your interview at this office on _____, I am pleased to offer you the above position with _____ ("the Company") subject to satisfactory references and a medical report. It is the Company's final decision as to whether such references meet with its requirements. You are advised not to resign from your present position until I have confirmed to you that your references have been received and are satisfactory to us. We will endeavour to obtain your references as quickly as possible.

If you accept this offer of employment, your job will be based at:

_____

Your employment will commence on _____ and the first four weeks will be treated as a probationary period during which time your employment may be terminated by yourself or by the Company on one week's notice.

Your duties and responsibilities will be as set out in the attached job description and you will be responsible to _____.

Your basic salary at the commencement of your employment will be £_____ per _____ payable monthly in arrears by bank credit transfer on the last day of each month. Your normal weekly hours will be from _____.

You will be entitled to ___ weeks holiday in every year, in addition to the normal statutory entitlement, of which no more than ___weeks may be taken consecutively. The holiday year runs from _____.

continued on next page

The Company will be entitled to terminate your appointment by giving you written notice of
_____.

You are required to give the Company _____week's notice of your intention to terminate your employment with the Company.

Your other terms of employment will be provided on your first day of employment.

If you wish to accept this offer of employment I would be grateful if you could confirm your acceptance by signing and returning one copy of this letter in the stamped addressed envelope enclosed.

I do hope that you will accept this offer. In the meantime, if you wish to discuss any aspect of this offer, please do not hesitate to contact me.

Yours sincerely,

_____
Personnel Manager

INTERVIEW CONFIRMATION

Date _____

To _____

_____

_____

Dear _____

This will confirm your appointment for an interview for the position of
_____.

The interview will be at our offices located at _____
at _____ m. You can expect the interview to take approximately_____ hours.

You will first meet_____
the_____. You are then scheduled to meet
_____.

After the interview, we will contact you regarding our decision.

Once again, thank you for your interest in our firm. We look forward to seeing you on the above
date.

Yours sincerely,

_____

Personnel Manager

INTERVIEW SCHEDULE

Date: _____ Time: _____

Applicant: _____ Position: _____

Comments: _____

_____

Date: _____ Time: _____

Applicant: _____ Position: _____

Comments: _____

_____

Date: _____ Time: _____

Applicant: _____ Position: _____

Comments: _____

_____

Date: _____ Time: _____

Applicant: _____ Position: _____

Comments: _____

_____

Date: _____ Time: _____

Applicant: _____ Position: _____

Comments: _____

_____

INTERVIEW SUMMARY

Applicant: _____ Phone: _____

Position/Department: _____

Interviewed by: _____ Date: _____

Available starting date: _____ Now employed? _____

Salary requested: _____

	Excellent	Good	Fair	Poor	N/A
Appearance:	_____	_____	_____	_____	_____
Experience:	_____	_____	_____	_____	_____
Education:	_____	_____	_____	_____	_____
Skills:	_____	_____	_____	_____	_____
Enthusiasm:	_____	_____	_____	_____	_____
Attitude:	_____	_____	_____	_____	_____
Other: _____	_____	_____	_____	_____	_____
Other: _____	_____	_____	_____	_____	_____

General comments/overall appraisal:

_____

_____

_____

_____

_____

_____

_____

Recommendation: Hire (   )   Reject (   )   Other(   ) _____

NO DECISION ON RECRUITMENT LETTER

Date _____

To _____

_____

_____

Dear _____

Thank you for your interest in employment with our company. You were among many well-qualified applicants who responded to our opening for a

Unfortunately, we have decided not to fill the position at this time.

We will keep your CV on file for six months and will contact you should we decide to fill this position within that period.

Thank you and good luck in your job search.

Yours sincerely,

_____

Personnel Manager

NOTIFICATION TO APPLICANT

Date _____

To _____

_____

_____

Dear _____

I am in receipt of your letter and cv in response to our advertisement for the position of _____. Thank you for your interest in our firm.

We have been unsuccessful in our attempts to reach you by telephone. I would be happy to discuss our job opening with you if you contact me at your earliest convenience at this telephone number _____.

I look forward to hearing from you.

Yours sincerely,

_____

RATING OF APPLICANT 1

Applicant: _____

Position/Department: _____

Interviewed by: _____ Date: _____

Job requirements:	Excellent	Good	Fair	Poor	N/A
_____	_____	_____	_____	_____	_____
_____	_____	_____	_____	_____	_____
_____	_____	_____	_____	_____	_____
_____	_____	_____	_____	_____	_____
_____	_____	_____	_____	_____	_____
_____	_____	_____	_____	_____	_____
_____	_____	_____	_____	_____	_____
_____	_____	_____	_____	_____	_____
_____	_____	_____	_____	_____	_____
_____	_____	_____	_____	_____	_____
_____	_____	_____	_____	_____	_____

General comments/Overall appraisal: _____

_____

_____

_____

_____

_____

Recommendation: Hire (   )   Reject (   )   Other(   ) _____

RATING OF APPLICANT 2

Applicant:_____

Position _____

Department _____

Use the following scale to rate applicant's qualifications:

5) Excellent   2) Below Average
4) Above Average   1) Unacceptable
3) Fully qualified 0) Unobserved

Education   _____

Experience   _____

Attention to detail   _____

Cooperation   _____

Initiative   _____

Integrity   _____

Interpersonal skills _____

Learning ability   _____

Stress tolerance   _____

Verbal communication _____

Overall:

_____Exceptional   _____Strong   _____Acceptable

_____Weak   _____Totally unacceptable

Recommendation:

_____Employ   _____Reject

_____Other _____

Signed:

_____   _____
Interviewer   Date

RATING OF APPLICANT: CLERICAL

Applicant: _____

Position/Department: _____

Interviewed by: _____ Date: _____

Office Skills:	Excellent	Good	Fair	Poor	N/A
Typing:	_____	_____	_____	_____	_____
Shorthand:	_____	_____	_____	_____	_____
Switchboard:	_____	_____	_____	_____	_____
P.C./Software:	_____	_____	_____	_____	_____
Telephone:	_____	_____	_____	_____	_____
Job Experience:	_____	_____	_____	_____	_____
Record of Job Success:	_____	_____	_____	_____	_____
Compatibility:	_____	_____	_____	_____	_____
Ability to Communicate:	_____	_____	_____	_____	_____
Ambition, Motivation:	_____	_____	_____	_____	_____
Other: _____	_____	_____	_____	_____	_____
Other: _____	_____	_____	_____	_____	_____

General comments/Overall appraisal: _____

_____

_____

_____

_____

_____

Recommendation: Hire (   )   Reject (   )   Other (   )_____

REJECTION LETTER 1

Date _____

To _____

_____

_____

Dear _____

Thank you for responding to our employment advertisement, and for coming to interview

on _____.

Your background and experience would certainly benefit many employers. However, we have selected another candidate who better meets our current requirements.

Thank you for your interest in the position and best wishes in your future endeavours.

Yours sincerely,

_____

Personnel Manager

REJECTION LETTER 2

Date _____

To _____

_____

_____

Dear _____

Thank you for coming for interview.

After careful deliberation, we have decided that another candidate for the position you applied for was better qualified for the job specifications. This does not reflect on your background or character. Those in our company who interviewed you were impressed with your experience and background.

We wish you luck in your career and thank you for your interest.

Yours sincerely,

_____

Personnel Manager

REJECTION LETTER 3

Date _____

To _____

_____

_____

Dear _____

Thank you for your inquiry about our recent advertisement for the position of

_____

We appreciate the opportunity to review your credentials and were pleased that you are interested in working with us.

We have narrowed our search to those few applicants who have the specific qualifications and experience we need for this position. Although your credentials do not specifically meet our current needs, we will retain your CV for six months, and in the event that an appropriate opportunity matching your background becomes available will contact you again.

Thank you again for your interest, and we wish you the best of luck in your search for employment.

Yours sincerely,

_____

Personnel Manager

REPLY TO APPLICANT

Date _____

To _____

_____

_____

Dear _____

Thank you for your inquiry regarding employment opportunities with our company.

Unfortunately, we do not anticipate any openings for _____

at the time you expect to graduate. However, we will retain the information you submitted for one year. Should an appropriate position open within that time, you will be contacted.

Your interest in our company is appreciated. We wish you success in your job search.

Yours sincerely,

_____
Personnel Manager

AUTHORISATION TO RELEASE INFORMATION

Date _____

To _____

_____

_____

Dear _____

I hereby authorise and request you to send the information ticked below to:

_____ the following party: _____

_____ any third party

The information to be released includes: (tick)

_____ Salary

_____ Position/department/section

_____ Date employment commenced

_____ Part-time/full-time or hours worked

_____ Garnishee orders or wage attachments, if any

_____ Reason for redundancy

_____ Medical/accident/illness reports

_____ Work performance rating

_____ Other: _____

Yours sincerely,

Employee Signature_____ Print Name _____

Address_____

Position or Title_____ Department _____

MEDICAL RECORDS REQUEST

Date _____

To _____

_____

Re National Insurance No.:

_____

Dear _____

_____ has applied to this company for

employment in the position of_____

_____

Because of the physical requirements this position entails, we request the following medical records:

_____

_____

_____

Please note the signature of the applicant granting permission below. Thank you for your co-operation.

Yours sincerely,

_____

I authorise release of all requested medical information to the above-listed requesting company.

_____   _____

Applicant's Signature   Date

MEDICAL TESTING AUTHORISATION

I, the undersigned, declare that I am a competent adult at least 18 years old. I hereby grant permission for the following medical test to be performed on me:

_____

_____

_____

_____

I further acknowledge that such tests may involve the temporary invasion or penetration of my body by medical instruments, light, sound, x-rays, or other imaging and diagnostic media, and may further involve the obtaining of bodily fluids, tissue, products or waste, all of which I give up any claim to.

I further certify that all such contemplated tests have been explained to me and that I have provided complete and honest responses to all questions posed to me regarding my health, including pregnancy, disabilities, allergies, and susceptibilities, if any.

I understand that these medical tests are not being performed for my benefit, but are instead performed for the benefit of _____which I hereby release from any and all responsibility for treatment, advice, referral, or diagnosis.

I grant this authorisation in exchange for the opportunity to be considered for employment, or for promotion in employment, and I acknowledge such testing is necessary and relevant to my employment.

I voluntarily make this grant without reservation.

_____   _____
Applicant   Date

_____   _____
Witness   Date

REFERENCE ACKNOWLEDGEMENT

Date _____

To _____

_____

Re _____

Dear _____

Thank you for your reference on the above individual. The applicant (   ) was (   ) was not offered a position with our firm, and your appraisal of the applicant's performance while employed with your firm was certainly an important factor in our decision.

We will hold your reference confidential unless you have authorised disclosure, and once again, we thank you for your cooperation, and would be pleased to reciprocate the courtesy.

Yours sincerely,

_____
Title

REFERENCE BY TELEPHONE CHECKLIST

Applicant: _____

Position applied for: _____

Person contacted: _____

Telephone: _____

Title: _____ Company: _____

Address: _____

_____ has applied for a position with us.

Would you please verify the following information?

• Dates of employment: From _____ To _____

• What was his or her position?

_____

_____

• Did he or she have supervisory responsibilities?

_____

_____

• How would you evaluate his or her work?

_____

_____

• Did the individual progress satisfactorily in the job?

_____

_____

• List his or her strong points.

_____

_____

• Were there any limitations?

_____

_____

REFERENCE BY TELEPHONE RECORD

Reference given on employee: _____

Date: _____ Time: _____

Person Inquiring: _____

Company: _____

Address: _____

_____ Phone: _____

Reason for inquiry: _____

_____

_____

Reference Summary:

_____

_____

_____

_____

_____

Specific Questions/Replies:

_____

_____

_____

_____

_____

_____

Submitted by

REFERENCE REQUEST BY APPLICANT

Date _____

From _____

_____

_____

To _____

_____

_____

I have applied for a job with _____

Address _____

_____

Contact _____

I have been asked to provide references to this potential employer to support my job application.

I would be grateful if you could write a reference on my behalf to the above Company based on your knowledge and experience of my work and character while under your employment.

Thank you in advance for your co-operation.

Yours sincerely,

_____

REFERENCE REQUEST BY EMPLOYER

Date _____

To _____

_____

_____

Re _____

Dear _____

The above named individual has applied for a position with our company and indicates previous employment with your firm. The information requested below will help us to evaluate the applicant. We will hold your comments in strict confidence. Thank you for your co-operation.

Yours sincerely,

_____

Personnel Department

Please indicate:

Position with your firm: _____

Employed from: _____ to _____

Final salary: £_____ Previous name(s): _____

Please rate the applicant on the basis of his or her employment with you (good/fair/poor):

Ability: _____ Conduct: _____ Attitude: _____

Efficiency: _____ Attendance: _____ Punctuality:_____

What was the reason for termination? _____

_____

Would you re-employ?_____. If not, please give reason:_____

_____

_____

Signature and Title

TRANSCRIPT REQUEST

Date _____

To _____

_____

_____

Please be advised that I am being considered for employment by

_____

and, in order to complete my application, they have requested a copy of my examinations certificates.

Please send a transcript to the following:

Firm: _____

Address: _____

_____

Attention:_____

Thank you.

Yours sincerely,

_____

Attended: _____ to _____
                     (month & year)   (month & year)

Degree/Diploma Received:_____

VERIFICATION OF BACKGROUND

Applicant name: _____ Date: _____

Position applied for: _____

Date of application: _____

	Requested	Received	Comments
Education/Schools:			
_____	_____	_____	_____
_____	_____	_____	_____
_____	_____	_____	_____
Prior employment:			
_____	_____	_____	_____
_____	_____	_____	_____
_____	_____	_____	_____
Military service:			
_____	_____	_____	_____
_____	_____	_____	_____
_____	_____	_____	_____
Other:			
_____	_____	_____	_____
_____	_____	_____	_____
_____	_____	_____	_____

Completed by _____

VERIFICATION OF EDUCATION

Date _____

To _____

_____

_____

Re _____

The above individual has applied to our organisation for employment.

According to the information in the employment application, this individual has attended your school/college. Would you please verify the above by completing the following information?

Dates attended _____

Still attending? _____

Degree/Diploma awarded_____

Honours or commendations_____

Other comments _____

_____

_____

_____

_____

Your co-operation in completing and returning this in the pre-paid envelope is greatly appreciated.

Yours sincerely,

_____
Personnel Manager

VERIFICATION OF EMPLOYMENT

Date _____

Ref (Applicant Name)

_____

Dear _____

The above individual is being evaluated for employment and has signed our employment application authorising this inquiry. We would appreciate a statement of your experiences with this person when employed by your company. Please provide the information requested on the bottom of this letter and return to us in the enclosed pre-paid envelope at your earliest convenience. Your reply will be held in strict confidence. We appreciate your cooperation and will gladly reciprocate.

Yours sincerely,

_____

CONFIDENTIAL

Applicant name _____

Address _____

Name of former company_____

Address _____

Employed from _____ to _____

General work record _____

_____

_____

_____

_____

Signed

VERIFICATION OF QUALIFICATION

Date _____

To _____

_____

_____

Dear _____

Please be advised that as a condition of my employment with _____

_____, I hereby authorise release of information

relative to the status of my qualification as a _____.

Please certify below and return to:

Firm _____

Address _____

_____

Attention _____

Thank you.

Yours sincerely,

_____

CERTIFICATION

This will certify that the above, _____,

is duly qualified as a _____ and the qualification is

in good standing with no disciplinary or revocation proceedings pending.

Dated: _____   _____
                                        Certifying Official

Section 2
Employee Introduction & Management

New Employees:

Announcement of New Employee – Announces the addition of a new employee.

Authorisation of Employment – Authorises hiring of personnel.

Checklist of New Employee – Lists information on employee to be in file before beginning work.

Checklist of New Personnel – Lists information to be obtained from new employee.

Data of New Employee – Records information about a new employee..

Job Description – Describes an employee's position, function, authority level and scope of work.

New Employee Letter 1 – Informs a new employee of the date to report to work.

New Employee Letter 2 – Welcomes a new employee.

New Employee Letter 3 – Informs a new employee of the date and time to report to work.

New Employee Letter 4 – Welcomes a new employee and informs him/her of the date and time to report to work.

Orientation Checklist – Lists information to be reviewed with new employees.

Personnel Management:

Annual Attendance Record - Employee's annual attendance record.

Drug/Alcohol Screen Testing Consent – Gives employee's permission to be tested for drug and alcohol use.

Drug Testing Memo - Informs employees of company's policy prohibiting drug use.

Emergency Telephone Numbers – Records emergency phone number information from a new employee.

Employee File – Records an employee's history with the company.

Employment Changes - Records any changes in employee's position and salary.

Health Record - Records an employee's illnesses and injuries that affect employment.

Information Release Consent - Authorises release of employment information.

Information Update - Requests employees to update information for personnel file.

Personnel Activity Report - Records the number of employees, salaries and positions during a given period.

Personnel Data Change - Records changes in an employee's address, marital status and number of dependents.

Personnel Data Sheet - Records changes in employee's salary and position with company.

Personnel File Access Log - Records access to personnel files.

Personnel File Inspection Request - Employee form to request inspection of file.

Personnel Requirement Projections - Projects personnel requirements for a given period.

Receipt for Company Property – Records company property issued to employee.

Receipt for Samples and Documents – Records samples and documents issued to employee.

Record of Employment - Records an employee's positions with the company.

Suggestion by Employee - Records suggestion for improving work conditions.

Suggestion Plan 1 - Outlines employee suggestion plan.

Suggestion Plan 2 - Outlines employee suggestion plan.

Transfer Request - Records employee's request for transfer.

Waiver of Liability – Releases company from any liability associated with employee's participation in company recreational activities.

Temporary Workers:

Acknowledgement of Temporary Employment – Employee acknowledges rights as a temporary employee.

Requisition of Temporary Employment - Requests employees for a temporary period.

Requisition of Temporary Personnel - Requests an employee for a temporary period.

ANNOUNCEMENT OF NEW EMPLOYEE

Date _____

To: all Employees

From _____

Subject: New Employee

I am pleased to announce that _____

has joined our staff as _____

In this new position, _____**will report to** _____

Our new employee comes to us from _____

where _____

and prior to that was _____

Please join me in welcoming _____

to our company and in wishing _____**much success!**

_____
Signed

AUTHORISATION OF EMPLOYMENT

Date _____

Applicant _____

Title/Job _____

_____

_____

P/T (　) F/T (　) Permanent (　) Temporary (　)

Starting salary £ _____ Starting date _____

Supervisor _____

Replacement (　) New Position (　)

Department _____ Budget _____

Description of duties _____

_____

_____

_____

Approval to employ is _____ granted

_____ not granted

Comments: _____

_____

_____

_____

_____

_____ By: _____

CHECKLIST OF NEW EMPLOYEE

Employee: _____ Position: _____

Department: _____ Starting date: _____

New employees must have ticked item(s) in file before beginning work.

Document	Required	Completed
Employment application	_____	_____
Personal data sheet	_____	_____
Employee verification sheet	_____	_____
Drug testing consent	_____	_____
Medical report	_____	_____
Employment contract	_____	_____
Non-Competition agreement	_____	_____
Confidentiality agreement	_____	_____
Conflict of interest declaration	_____	_____
Indemnity agreement	_____	_____
Security clearance	_____	_____
Other:		
_____	_____	_____
_____	_____	_____
_____	_____	_____

_____

Supervisor

_____

Date

CHECKLIST OF NEW PERSONNEL

_____Employment application

_____ Reference reports

_____ Formal job offer letter and employee acknowledgement

_____ Employment contract, confidentiality agreement

_____ Verification of citizenship or employment status

_____ Inland Revenue tax forms

_____ Insurance forms: health, group life, disability

_____ Physical examination reports

_____ Security records.

_____ Performance evaluations

_____ Retirement plan application

_____ Receipt for benefit plan options and elections

_____ Termination agreement and exit interview

DATA OF NEW EMPLOYEE

Name:_____

Employee Identification No.: _____

Address: _____

Position:_____ Department:_____

Pay frequency: _____ Pay code: _____ Annual salary: _____

Employment date: _____ Employment code: _____ Cost centre: _____

Sex: _____ M _____ F

Marital Status:

_____ Single_____ Married _____ Separated _____Widowed _____Divorced

Birth date: _____ Home tel:_____

Spouse's name: _____

Children

Name: _____ Birth date: _____

Name: _____ Birth date: _____

Name: _____ Birth date: _____

Name: _____ Birth date: _____

Education

High School:_____ No. of Yrs :_____ Degree:_____

College:_____ No. of Yrs :_____ Degree:_____

Post-Graduate:_____ No. of Yrs :_____ Degree:_____

Military Service: Branch_____ Rank _____ Discharge Date _____

Emergency Notification

Name:_____

Phone: _____ Relationship: _____

Address: _____

JOB DESCRIPTION

Position: _____

_____

_____

Basic function: _____

_____

_____

Scope of work: _____

_____

_____

Principal accountabilities: _____

_____

_____

_____

Principal interactions: _____

_____

_____

_____

Knowledge/Educational requirements: _____

_____

_____

_____

Authority level: _____

_____

_____

Reports to: _____

_____

_____

NEW EMPLOYEE LETTER 1

Date _____

To _____

_____

_____

Dear _____

This acknowledges your acceptance of our employment offer. We are pleased you have decided to join our company and look forward to you joining us on _____. As discussed, we will pay your moving and travel expenses according to company policy. We will make the necessary arrangement to move your furniture with a removal firm. Please submit your personal transportation expenses to us at the time you report for work.

Again, we are happy you have made the decision to accept our offer. Please do not hesitate to let us know if we can assist you in any way.

Yours sincerely,

_____

NEW EMPLOYEE LETTER 2

Date _____

To _____

_____

_____

Dear _____

It is a pleasure to welcome you as a new member of _____.

You are now part of _____.

As you become more familiar with your duties and better acquainted with the other members of our company, you will find that all of us have an important part to play.

My warmest wishes to you on beginning your employment with us.

Yours sincerely,

_____

NEW EMPLOYEE LETTER 3

Date _____

To _____

_____

_____

Dear _____

At _____m, on _____, please report for work
at the personnel office of _____.
We hope you are looking forward to this event as enthusiastically as we are.

You are now a member of a fine group of people operating as a team with the common objective
of providing _____

We are very happy that you have chosen us at this stage in your career. We look forward to seeing
you on your starting day.

Yours sincerely,

_____

NEW EMPLOYEE LETTER 4

Date _____

To _____

_____

_____

Dear _____

Your new position with our company will begin on _____,at_____.
We welcome you with pleasure.

This is an opportunity to establish and develop a mutually rewarding relationship. It is with great confidence that we look forward to achieving this goal.

If you have any questions, please let us know.

Yours sincerely,

_____

ORIENTATION CHECKLIST

Employee: _____ Position: _____

Starting Date: _____ Interview date: _____

Supervisor: _____

	To be reviewed (Tick)	Reviewed (Tick)
Conditions of employment	_____	_____
Probationary period	_____	_____
Union memberships	_____	_____
Work schedule	_____	_____
Holidays	_____	_____
Attendance & absences	_____	_____
Payroll procedures	_____	_____
Parking	_____	_____
Lunch break schedule	_____	_____
Cafeteria facilities	_____	_____
Health and Safety	_____	_____
Advancement opportunities	_____	_____
Group insurance	_____	_____
Life insurance	_____	_____
Grievance procedures	_____	_____
Day care	_____	_____
Cafeteria plans	_____	_____
General fringe benefits	_____	_____
Health insurance	_____	_____
Pension/Retirement	_____	_____
Training reimbursement	_____	_____
Changes in personnel records	_____	_____
Employee policy information	_____	_____

continued on next page

Employee Received:

Union information   _____

Safety rules   _____

Grievance procedure   _____

Group insurance information   _____

Life insurance Information   _____

Medical insurance information   _____

Employee policy   _____

Other: _____

_____   _____

_____

_____

_____

Personnel Representative

_____

Date

I acknowledge that the above ticked items have been discussed to my satisfaction, and I also acknowledge receipt of the items ticked.

_____

Employee

_____

Date

ANNUAL ATTENDANCE RECORD
FOR CALENDAR YEAR _____

Employee: _____ Employee No.: _____

Position: _____ Department: _____

Day	Jan	Feb	Mar	Apr	May	Jun	Jul	Aug	Sep	Oct	Nov	Dec
1												
2												
3												
4												
5												
6												
7												
8												
9												
10												
11												
12												
13												
14												
15												
16												
17												
18												
19												
20												
21												
22												
23												
24												
25												
26												
27												
28												
29												
30												
31												

A = Absent   O = Other   B = Bank Holiday   P = Personal Leave Approved

S = Sick   L = Late   F = Funeral Leave   U = Unauthorised Absence

J = Jury Service I = Job Injury   H = Holiday   LO = Leave of Absence

Comments and summary of attendance: _____

_____

_____

DRUG/ALCOHOL SCREEN TESTING CONSENT

I , _____,
have been fully informed by my potential employer of the reasons for this urine test for drug
and/or alcohol. I understand what I am being tested for, the procedure involved, and do hereby
freely give my consent. In addition, I understand that the results of this test will be forwarded to
my potential employer and become part of my record.

If this test result is positive and for this reason I am not offered employment, I understand that I
will be given the opportunity to explain the results of this test.

I hereby authorise these test results to be released to:

_____

_____

_____

_____   _____
Signature   Date

_____   _____
Witness   Date

DRUG TESTING MEMO

To: All Employees

From: Personnel

Subject: Drug Testing

Our company has a rigorous policy against the use, sale, or possession of illegal drugs on company property. We intend to enforce this policy strictly.

We have strong reason to believe that some employees are using drugs at work. While we hope this is not the case, we want to advise all employees that we plan to carry out a thorough investigation of any suspected drug use or sale on our property. Our investigation may include drug testing through urine analysis and/or the use of undercover detectives.

We certainly don't want to use such drastic measures, but we will have no choice if we find reasonable evidence of drug activity.

We believe there are better ways to overcome drug abuse than investigation and prosecution. Therefore, we have engaged external consultants called_____ to draw up and implement an Employee Assistance Plan (EAP). You can seek advice and treatment as part of this EAP should you need it; the company will pay for any advice and treatment as long as you adhere to the recommended programme, and stay off drugs. Getting onto this confidential programme, may save your job and your life. Call   .

_____
Signed

EMERGENCY TELEPHONE NUMBERS

Employee: _____ Date: _____

In the event of a medical emergency, the following people and emergency medical personnel should be contacted:

Contact 1: _____

Telephone: _____

Relationship:_____

Contact 2: _____

Telephone: _____

Relationship:_____

Doctor:_____

Telephone: _____

Medical Card No.: _____

_____

Health/Medical History:_____

_____

Medication taken and allergies:_____

_____

Please complete and return to the Personnel Department.

EMPLOYEE FILE

Employee: _____

Address: _____

Phone: _____ National Insurance No.: _____

DOB: _____ Sex: _____M _____F

Marital Status:

_____ Single _____ Married _____ Separated _____ Widowed _____ Divorced

Name of Spouse: _____ No. Dependents _____

In Emergency Notify: _____

Address: _____

_____

Education

Secondary School _____ Years: _____

University/College _____ Years: _____

Other _____ Years: _____

Employment History

Date From /To	Position	Salary
_____	_____	£ _____
_____	_____	£ _____
_____	_____	£ _____
_____	_____	£ _____
_____	_____	£ _____
_____	_____	£ _____

Dismissal Information

Date dismissed: _____ Would we re-employ? ___ Yes ___ No

Reason for dismissal: _____

_____

_____

EMPLOYMENT CHANGES

Employee: _____ Employment Date: _____

Department: _____ Supervisor: _____

Effective Date: _____ Date Submitted: _____

1.   Pay Rate Change:

     From: _____ to _____

2.   Position Title Change:

     From: _____ to _____

3.   Position Classification Change:

     From: _____ to _____

4.   Shift Change:

     From: _____ to _____

5.   Full-Time/Part-Time Change:

     From: _____ to _____

6.   Temporary/Permanent Change:

     From: _____ to _____

7.   Other: (Describe)

     _____

     _____

_____   _____
Submitted By   Date

_____   _____
Approved By   Date

HEALTH RECORD

Name:_____

Address: _____

_____ Phone: _____

Date Employed: _____ Position: _____

Sex:_____ Age: _____ Date of Pre-Employment Medical: _____

Doctor: _____ Phone: _____

Medical History (Allergies, Restrictions, etc.): _____

_____

_____

_____

In Emergency, Notify:_____ Relationship: _____

Address: _____

_____ Phone: _____

Date	Time	Illness/Injury	Treatment/Action
_____	_____	_____	_____
_____	_____	_____	_____
_____	_____	_____	_____
_____	_____	_____	_____
_____	_____	_____	_____
_____	_____	_____	_____
_____	_____	_____	_____
_____	_____	_____	_____
_____	_____	_____	_____

_____   _____

Employee Signature   Date

INFORMATION RELEASE CONSENT

To _____

From: Personnel Office

A request for verification of employment information has been received from:

_____

Please tick below those items for which information may be released.

_____ Salary

_____ Position

_____ Department

_____ Supervisor

_____ Health records

_____ Dates of employment

_____ Part-time/Full-time

_____ Hours worked

_____ Whether you work under a maiden name

_____ Wage attachments

_____ Other:

_____   _____
Employee Signature   Date

Please return this form to the Personnel Dept. as soon as possible. Your consent on this occasion will not constitute a consent to release on future occasions.

INFORMATION UPDATE

To All Employees:

Please print all information.

Name:_____

Street address: _____

Town: _____

Post code: _____

Telephone number:_____

Marital status:_____

Name of spouse: _____

Number of dependants: _____

Emergency contact: _____

Emergency telephone number: _____

PERSONNEL ACTIVITY REPORT

Period from: _____ to: _____

Date prepared: _____ Prepared by: _____

	Salaried	Hourly	Part-time
No. employees at start of period	_____	_____	_____
No. employees at end of period	_____	_____	_____
No. positions presently open	_____	_____	_____
No. applicants interviewed	_____	_____	_____
No. applicants hired	_____	_____	_____
% applicants hired during period	_____	_____	_____
No. employees terminated	_____	_____	_____
No. employees resigned	_____	_____	_____
No. openings at start of period	_____	_____	_____
No. openings at end of period	_____	_____	_____
Total requisitions to be filled	_____	_____	_____
Requisitions received	_____	_____	_____
Requisitions filled	_____	_____	_____
Requisitions unfilled	_____	_____	_____
Turnover rate for period	_____	_____	_____
Other: _____	_____	_____	_____
_____	_____	_____	_____

Notes: _____

_____

_____

_____

_____

PERSONNEL DATA CHANGE

Employee: _____ Employment Date: _____

Department: _____ Supervisor: _____

Effective Date: _____ Employee No.: _____

Change/Update Employee Personnel File as follows:

Name (Marital) Change:_____

New Address: _____

New Telephone No.: _____

Marital Status: _____

Number of Dependants: _____

Other:_____

_____

_____

_____

_____

_____   _____
Employee   Date

_____   _____
Supervisor   Date

PERSONNEL DATA SHEET

Employee:_____

Employment date: _____ Employee No.: _____

Address: _____

_____ Tel: _____

New Address: _____

_____ Tel: _____

Emergency Contact:_____ Tel: _____

Marital Status: _____ Spouse Name: _____

Type of Personnel Change	Date	Pay Increase	Merit/Promotion/Other
_____	_____	_____	_____
_____	_____	_____	_____
_____	_____	_____	_____
_____	_____	_____	_____
_____	_____	_____	_____
_____	_____	_____	_____
_____	_____	_____	_____
_____	_____	_____	_____
_____	_____	_____	_____
_____	_____	_____	_____
_____	_____	_____	_____
_____	_____	_____	_____
_____	_____	_____	_____
_____	_____	_____	_____
_____	_____	_____	_____
_____	_____	_____	_____
_____	_____	_____	_____

PERSONNEL FILE ACCESS LOG

Employee:_____

Employee Number:_____

THIS FILE MUST REMAIN WITH THE PERSONNEL DEPARTMENT.

Notice: All medical information and pre-employment references will be removed from this file prior to any review.

Date	Name	Reason for Review

PERSONNEL FILE INSPECTION REQUEST

Employee: _____ Date Requested: _____

Employee Number:_____

Department/Location: _____

Work Tel: _____

I request an appointment with the Personnel Department for the purpose of inspecting my personnel file.

I previously reviewed my file: _____

_____   _____
Signature   Date

File review appointment scheduled for:

Date: _____ Time: _____

Location: _____

Date File Review completed: _____

Employee comments regarding information in the personnel file:

_____

_____

_____

_____

_____   _____
Personnel Representative   Date

_____   _____
Employee Signature   Date

Employee should complete top section of request form and forward to the Personnel Department. Place one completed copy of this form into personnel file upon completion of review.

PERSONNEL REQUIREMENT PROJECTIONS

Period from: _____ to _____

Number of personnel required at end of time period:_____

Number employed now: _____

Loss of personnel:

Retirement:_____

Death:_____

Dismissal:_____

Resignation:_____

Promotion:_____

Lay-Off:_____

Redundancy:_____

Transfer:_____

Total personnel loss
during time period:_____

Gain of personnel:

New hires (routine):_____

Promoted in:_____

Training graduates:_____

Additional personnel required:_____

_____   _____
Submitted By   Date

RECEIPT FOR COMPANY PROPERTY

Employee:_____

Identification No.: _____

Department/Section: _____

I hereby acknowledge receipt of the company property listed below. I agree to keep the property in good condition and to return it when I leave the company, or earlier on request. I agree to report immediately any loss or damage to the property. In addition, I agree to use the property only for work-related purposes.

Item: _____ Received From:_____ Date: _____

Serial No.:_____ Returned To: _____ Date: _____

Item: _____ Received From:_____ Date: _____

Serial No.:_____ Returned To: _____ Date: _____

Item: _____ Received From:_____ Date: _____

Serial No.:_____ Returned To: _____ Date: _____

Item: _____ Received From:_____ Date: _____

Serial No.:_____ Returned To: _____ Date: _____

Item: _____ Received From:_____ Date: _____

Serial No.:_____ Returned To: _____ Date: _____

Item: _____ Received From:_____ Date: _____

Serial No.:_____ Returned To: _____ Date: _____

_____

Employee

_____

Date

RECEIPT FOR SAMPLES AND DOCUMENTS

I, _____, employed in the position
of_____, confirm
that I have received from my employer the following samples:

No. Rec'd.	Serial No.	Description	Value Each	Total value
_____	_____	_____	_____	_____
_____	_____	_____	_____	_____
_____	_____	_____	_____	_____
_____	_____	_____	_____	_____
_____	_____	_____	_____	_____

In addition I confirm that I have received the following documents:

_____

_____

_____

_____

I accept responsibility to safeguard these materials, prevent the disclosure of confidential material and return these (except those authorised for and delivered to customers) to my employer upon demand and, in any event, upon termination of employment.

_____
Employee

_____
Date

RECORD OF EMPLOYMENT

Employee: _____

Employee number: _____

Date	Department	Position	Rate	Per	Comments
_____	_____	_____	_____	_____	_____
_____	_____	_____	_____	_____	_____
_____	_____	_____	_____	_____	_____
_____	_____	_____	_____	_____	_____
_____	_____	_____	_____	_____	_____
_____	_____	_____	_____	_____	_____
_____	_____	_____	_____	_____	_____
_____	_____	_____	_____	_____	_____
_____	_____	_____	_____	_____	_____
_____	_____	_____	_____	_____	_____
_____	_____	_____	_____	_____	_____
_____	_____	_____	_____	_____	_____
_____	_____	_____	_____	_____	_____
_____	_____	_____	_____	_____	_____
_____	_____	_____	_____	_____	_____
_____	_____	_____	_____	_____	_____
_____	_____	_____	_____	_____	_____
_____	_____	_____	_____	_____	_____
_____	_____	_____	_____	_____	_____
_____	_____	_____	_____	_____	_____

Submitted by:_____ Date: _____

Approved by: _____ Date: _____

SUGGESTION BY EMPLOYEE

Employee: _____ Position: _____

Department: _____ Tel No.: _____

Is this a group submittal? Yes (   )   No (   )

(If yes, list all members of this group here, and obtain their signatures on the reverse side.)

_____

_____

_____

_____

What is the problem? Be specific.

_____

_____

_____

_____

What do you propose to improve this situation or problem? Be specific. Attach samples if applicable.

_____

_____

_____

_____

What benefits, savings and implementation costs can be expected from this solution? How did you calculate these savings?

_____

_____

_____

_____

I have read and understand the rules and regulations governing the Suggestion System and agree to be bound by them. I understand that the company has the sole discretion to make an award or not, and that it may use a suggestion without giving an award.

_____   _____
Employee   Date

SUGGESTION PLAN 1

Suggestion boxes are located throughout the company premises. These boxes contain suggestion forms to fill out when you have an idea you think has merit.

The idea may reduce costs, improve the quality of our products, or positively change a method. It may eliminate a dangerous hazard, reduce waste, change a handling procedure or improve housekeeping.

If approved, suggestions may receive awards according to the value of the idea. The suggestions are held on file for seven years.

The Suggestion Plan allows you to express your interest, ingenuity, and initiative. We hope you will use it frequently. Fill out a suggestion blank and put it in the office mail. Your idea will receive prompt acknowledgement and investigation and, if approved, an award.

Yours sincerely,

_____

Suggestion Office

SUGGESTION PLAN 2

The company Suggestion Plan enables you to make any suggestions for the benefit of everyone.

Give your suggestion to your immediate supervisor, who will see that it gets to the Evaluating Committee.

Your suggestion can help eliminate unnecessary expenses and squeeze more value out of every overhead pound.

If the Evaluating Committee accepts your suggestion, you will be rewarded based on the suggestion's value to the company.

Look around the workplace. Review each procedure and routine in your daily tasks. Ask yourself: is there a more cost-effective way of doing this? Is there a way to streamline this job? Is there a way to improve quality and accuracy? If you think so, submit your idea. We value your suggestions.

Yours sincerely,

_____
Suggestion Office

TRANSFER REQUEST

Employee: _____ Supervisor: _____

Department: _____ Shift: _____

Present Position: _____ Starting Date: _____

Requested Position: _____

Related Experience: _____

Reason for transfer request: _____

_____

_____

_____ _____
Employee   Date

Supervisor's Comments

Evaluation in present position: _____

_____

_____

Recommended action: _____

_____

_____ _____
Supervisor   Date

Action Taken

Date received: _____ Date interviewed: _____ Time:_____

Comments:_____

_____

Action: _____

Date employee notified: _____

_____ _____
Interviewer Signature   Date

WAIVER OF LIABILITY

I,_____ (Employee),
hereby release _____ (Company)
from any and all liability connected with my participation in company recreational activities. I acknowledge that I am participating in these activities in my own time and at my own election and hereby assume all risk in connection therewith.

_____
Employee

_____
Date

_____
Witness

ACKNOWLEDGEMENT OF TEMPORARY EMPLOYMENT

I, the undersigned, understand I am being employed by_____

_____(Company) in a temporary position only and for such time as my services are required. I hereby acknowledge that this temporary employment does not entitle me to any special consideration for permanent employment. I further understand that subject to law my temporary employment may be terminated at any time following the usual disciplinary procedures applicable to permanent employees. Furthermore, I understand that I am not eligible to participate in any retirement benefits or any other benefits available to permanent employees (unless required by law) and in the event that I am allowed to participate in any benefit, then my continued participation may be withdrawn or terminated by the Company at any time and without reason.

_____
Employee

_____
Date

_____
Witness

REQUISITION OF TEMPORARY EMPLOYMENT

Date _____

To _____

Number of Temporary Employees Needed: _____

Position/Duties: _____

Department: _____

Supervisor: _____

Starting Dates: _____ to _____

Shift _____ to _____

Reasons for Requisition: _____

_____

_____

_____

_____

_____

Estimated Cost: _____

Budget Number: _____

Budgeted?   Yes _____   No _____

_____   _____
Signed By   Date

_____   _____
Approved By   Date

Temporary personnel are not allowed employment beyond approval period or for an amount above estimated expense, unless approved in advance.

REQUISITION OF TEMPORARY PERSONNEL

Job Title: _____ Full Time: _____ Part Time: _____

Supervisor: _____ Department: _____

Dates Desired: from: _____ to _____

Hours Desired: from: _____ to _____

Reason for Employment: _____

_____

_____

_____

_____

_____

_____

_____

Job Description: _____

_____

_____

_____

_____

_____

_____

_____

_____

_____   _____
Supervisor's Signature   Date

_____   _____
Approved By   Date

Section 3
Employment Terms

Agreements & Procedures:

Confidentiality Agreement – Employee agrees to keep information about company and employees confidential.

Conflict of Interest Declaration – A declaration by an employee that his personal affairs do not conflict with his duty to his employer.

Contract of Employment – Agreement with employee outlining standard terms and conditions of employment.

Covenants of Employee – Employee agrees to be liable for any disclosure of trade secrets or solicitation or promotion of another company similar to employer.

Emergency Procedures – Describes steps to take in particular emergencies.

Independent Contractor's Agreement – Contract for services from an independent contractor.

Inventions and Patents Agreement – Employee agrees to non-disclosure of company information regarding inventions and patents.

Non-Competition Agreement – Employee agrees to not compete with employer for a specified period upon termination.

Sales Representative Agreement – Contract with sales representative outlining terms of contract.

Sales Representative Agreement: Change in Terms – Changes terms of an existing sales representative agreement.

Sales Representative Agreement Extension – Extends length of contract by a specified time.

Staff Handbook - Includes an Equal Opportunities Policy, Health & Safety Policy, Data Protection Policy, Whistleblowing Policy, Disciplinary Rules & Procedure and Grievance Procedure.

Terms of Employment Changes – Changes or adds provisions to an existing agreement.

Terms of Employment Summary – Summarises terms of employment.

Payroll:

Direct Deposit Authorisation – Authorises direct deposit of an employee's pay cheque.

Pay Advice - Summarises am employee's deductions and gross and net pay for a given payroll period.

Pay or Grade Change Following Job Evaluation – Records salary change resulting from an evaluation.

Payroll Change Notice - Notifies payroll department of a change in payroll.

Payroll for Department - Records employees' regular and overtime hours or wages for a specific department and period.

Salary Change Request – Records salary increase recommendation.

Salary Deduction Authorisation – Authorises specific deductions from an employee's pay cheque.

Salary Deduction Direct Deposit Authorisation – Authorises direct deposit of a specific payroll deduction.

Salary Record - Records history of employee's salary and positions with company.

Salary Rise: Letter to Employee – A letter to employee informing of increase in salary.

Working Hours:

Flexitime Schedule - Records an employee's schedule.

Night Work Acceptance Agreement – Makes night work a condition of employment with company.

Overtime Authorisation - Authorises specified overtime for a specified employee.

Overtime Report: Individual - Records total hours and total salaries for a specific department during a specific payroll period.

Overtime Report: Departmental - Records employees' overtime hours in a specific department for a specific period.

Overtime Request: Departmental - Requests a specific amount of overtime for specified employees.

Time Record: Daily 1 - Records employees' hours for a given day.

Time Record: Daily 2 - Records an employee's daily hours over a specified period.

Time Sheet: Weekly - Records employees' daily and weekly hours for a given week.

Work Schedule: Weekly - Establishes employees' schedules for a given week.

Working Time Regulations Opt Out Agreement – agreement whereby employee agrees not to be bound to Working Time Regulations.

CONFIDENTIALITY AGREEMENT

THIS AGREEMENT is made the _____ day of _____ year _____

BETWEEN:

(1) _____ (the "Company"); and

(2) _____ (the "Employee").

WHEREAS:

(A) The Company agrees to give the Employee access to certain confidential information relating to the affairs of the Company solely for purposes of:

_____

_____

_____

_____

(B) The Employee agrees to obtain, inspect and use such information only for the purposes described above, and otherwise to hold such information confidential and secret pursuant to the terms of this agreement.

NOW IT IS HEREBY AGREED as follows:

1. The Company has or shall furnish to the Employee confidential information, described on the attached list, and may further allow suppliers, customers, employees or representatives of the Company to disclose information to the Employee.

2. The Employee agrees to hold all confidential or proprietary information or trade secrets ("Information") in trust and confidence and agrees that the Information shall be used only for the contemplated purpose, and not for any other purpose or disclosed to any third party under any circumstances whatsoever.

3. No copies may be made or retained of the Information.

4. At the conclusion of our discussions, or upon demand by the Company, all Information, including written notes, photographs, or memoranda shall be promptly returned to the Company. The Employee shall retain no copies or written documentation relating thereto.

5. This Information shall not be disclosed to any employee, consultant or third party unless that third party agrees to execute and be bound by the terms of this agreement, and disclosure by the Company is first approved.

continued on next page

6. It is understood that the Employee shall have no obligation with respect to any information known by the Employee, or as may be generally known within the industry, prior to date of this agreement, or that shall become common knowledge within the industry thereafter.

7. The Employee acknowledges the Information disclosed herein contains proprietary or trade secrets and in the event of any breach, the Company shall be entitled to apply for injunctive relief and to claim for damages of breach.

8. This agreement shall be binding upon and inure to the benefit of the parties, their successors and assigns.

9. This constitutes the entire agreement.

IN WITNESS OF WHICH the parties have signed this agreement the day and year first above written

Signed for and on behalf of the Company

_____

Director

_____

Director/Secretary

_____

Signed by or on behalf of the Employee

_____

in the presence of (witness)

_____

Name

_____

Address

_____

_____

Occupation

CONFLICT OF INTEREST DECLARATION

Employee _____

Company _____

I acknowledge that I have read the Company policy statement concerning conflicts of interest and I hereby declare that neither I, nor any other business to which I may be associated, nor, to the best of my knowledge, any member of my immediate family has any conflict between our personal affairs or interests and the proper performance of my responsibilities for the Company that would constitute a violation of that Company policy. Furthermore, I declare that during my employment, I shall continue to maintain my affairs in accordance with the requirements of said policy.

_____
Employee's Signature

_____
Date

CONTRACT OF EMPLOYMENT

THIS AGREEMENT IS MADE the _____ day of _____ year _____

BETWEEN

(1) _____(the "Employer");and

(2) _____ (the "Employee").

This document sets out the terms and conditions of employment which are required to be given to the Employee under section 1 Employment Rights Act 1996 and which apply at the date hereof.

1. **Commencement and Job Title:** The Employer agrees to employ the Employee from _____ _____ year _____ in the capacity of _____ at _____.

    [No employment with a previous employer will be counted as part of the Employee's period of continuous employment][The employment under this Agreement forms part of a continuous period of employment which began on _____]. The Employee's duties which this job entails are set out in the job description attached to this statement. The job description may from time to time be reasonably modified as necessary to meet the needs of the Employer's business.

2. **Salary:** The Employer shall pay the Employee a salary of £_____ per year payable by credit transfer at [weekly] [monthly] intervals on _____. The Company shall review the Employee's salary at such intervals as it shall at its sole discretion decide.

3. **Hours of Employment:** The Employee's normal hours of employment shall be _____ to _____ on Mondays to Fridays [and _____ to _____ on Saturdays] during which time the Employee may take up to one hour for lunch between the hours of ___pm and ___pm, and the Employee may from time to time be required to work such additional hours as is reasonable to meet the requirements of the Employer's business [at no additional payment] [at an overtime rate of £ _____ per hour].

4. **Holidays:** The Employee shall be entitled to _____ days holiday per calendar year at full pay in addition to the normal public holidays. Holidays must be taken at a time that is convenient to the Employer and sufficient notice of intention to take holiday must be given to the Employee's supervisor. No more than _____ weeks' holiday may be taken at any one time unless permission is given by the Employee's supervisor.

    [The Employee shall be entitled to payment in lieu of holiday accrued due but untaken at the date of termination of his or her employment. If at the date of termination the Employee has

continued on next page

taken holiday in excess of his or her accrued entitlement a corresponding deduction will be made from his or her final payment].

5. **Sickness:** If the Employee is absent from work on account of sickness or injury, he or she or someone on his or her behalf should inform the employer of the reason for the absence as soon as possible but no later than _____am/pm on the working day on which absence first occurs.

    [The Company reserves the right to ask the Employee at any stage of absence to produce a medical certificate and/or to undergo a medical examination].

    The Employee shall be paid normal remuneration during sickness absence for a maximum of _____ weeks in any period of ___ months provided that the Employee provides the Employer with a medical certificate in the case of absence of more than ___ consecutive days. Such remuneration will be less the amount of any Statutory Sick Pay or Social Security sickness benefits to which the Employee may be entitled. Entitlement to payment is subject to notification of absence and production of medical certificates as required above.

6. **Collective Agreements:** [There are no collective agreements in force directly relating to the terms of your employment] [The terms of the collective agreement dated _____ made between _____ and _____ shall deemed to be included in this Agreement].

7. **Pension:** [There is no pension scheme applicable to the Employee] [The Employee shall be entitled to join the Employer's pension scheme the details of which are set out in the Employer's booklet/leaflet entitled _____ and which is available on request]. A contracting-out certificate under the Pension Schemes Act 1993 [is][is not] in force in respect of this employment.

8. **Termination:** The Employer may terminate this Agreement by giving written notice to the Employee as follows:

    (a) with not less than one week's notice during the first two years of continuous employment; then

    (b) with not less than a further one week's notice for each full year of continuous employment after the first two years until the twelfth year of continuous employment; and

    (c) with not less than twelve weeks' notice after twelve years of continuous employment.

    The Employer may terminate this Agreement without notice or payment in lieu of notice in the case of serious or persistent misconduct such as to cause a major breach of the Employer's disciplinary rules.

    The Employee may terminate this Agreement by one week's written notice to the Employer.

    After notice of termination has been given by either party, the Employer may in its absolute

continued on next page

discretion give the Employee payments in lieu of all or any part of any notice; or, provided the Employee continues to be paid and to enjoy his or her full contractual benefits under the terms of this Agreement, the Employer may in its absolute discretion for all or part of the notice period exclude the Employee from the premises of the Employer and require that he or she carries out duties other than those specified in his or her job description or require that he or she carries out no duties at all until the termination of his or her employment.

9. **Confidentiality:** The Employee is aware that during his or her employment he may be party to confidential information concerning the Employer and the Employer's business. The Employee shall not during the term of this employment disclose or allow the disclosure of any confidential information (except in the proper course of his employment).

   After the termination of this Agreement the Employee shall not disclose or use any of the Employer's trade secrets or any other information which is of a sufficiently high degree of confidentiality to amount to a trade secret. The Employer shall be entitled to apply for an injunction to prevent such disclosure or use and to seek any other remedy including without limitation the recovery of damages in the case of such disclosure or use.

   The obligation of confidentiality both during and after the termination of this Agreement shall not apply to any information which the Employee is enabled to disclose under the Public Interest Disclosure Act 1998 provided the Employee has first fully complied with the Employer's procedures relating to such external disclosures.

10. **Non-Competition:** For a period of [_____ months] [_____ year(s)] after the termination of this Agreement the Employee shall not solicit or seek business from any customers or clients of the Employer who were customers or clients of the Employer at any time during the _____ [months] [year(s)] immediately preceding the termination of this Agreement.

11. **Discipline and Grievance:** The Employer's disciplinary rules and procedure and the grievance and appeal procedure in connection with these rules are set out in the Employer's Staff Handbook which is attached hereto.

12. **Notices:** All communications including notices required to be given under this Agreement shall be in writing and shall be sent either by personal service or first class post to the parties' respective addresses.

13. **Severability:** If any provision of this Agreement should be held to be invalid it shall to that extent be severed and the remaining provisions shall continue to have full force and effect.

14. **Staff Handbook:** Further details of the arrangements affecting your employment are published in the Staff Handbook as issued and/or amended from time to time. These are largely of an administrative nature but, so far as relevant, are to be treated as incorporated in this Agreement.

continued on next page

15. Governing Law: This Agreement shall be construed in accordance with the laws of England and Wales and shall be subject to the exclusive jurisdiction of the English courts.

Please acknowledge receipt of this statement and your agreement to the terms set out in it by signing the attached copy of this letter and returning it to _____.

IN WITNESS OF WHICH the parties hereto have signed this Agreement the day and year first above written

SIGNED   _____   _____

       Signed by or on behalf of the Employer   in the presence of (witness)

       Name _____

       Address _____

       _____

       DATED _____   Occupation _____

SIGNED   _____   _____

       Signed by the Employee   in the presence of (witness)

       Name _____

       Address _____

       _____

       DATED _____   Occupation _____

COVENANTS OF EMPLOYEE

_____ (Employee), a resident
of _____ and employed by or about
to be employed by_____(Company),
hereby makes these covenants to Company in consideration for_____
____ hiring Employee in the position of_____
____ continued employment of Employee, with the following change in the nature
    of employment _____

COVENANT 1

Employee's Covenants

During the term of employment and one (1) year after termination, Employee agrees to refrain from the following:

1. Promoting or engaging in indirectly or directly, as an employee, principal, partner, contractor, associate, agent, manager or otherwise, or by means of any entity, any business in the same or similar business as Company or its affiliates within the following geographic area:

_____

_____

_____

_____

2. Soliciting Company's customers, employees, staff, vendors, subcontractors, or prospects with services or products of the nature of those being sold by Company or affiliates of Company.

3. Employee agrees Company and its affiliates hold certain trade, business, and financial secrets in connection with the business. Employee covenants to not divulge to any party at any time, directly or indirectly, during the term of this Agreement or afterwards, unless directed by the Board of Directors, any information acquired by Employee about Company or its affiliates, including, but not limited to, customer lists, trade secrets, documents, financial statements, quotes, correspondence, patents, processes, formulas, research, intellectual property, expenses, costs or other confidential information of any kind, or any other data that could be used by third parties to the disadvantage of Company. This paragraph shall survive the term of employment.

continued on next page

COVENANT 2

Company Rights on Breach

If Employee breaches this covenant, Company shall have the right, in addition to all other rights available hereunder and by law, to enjoin Employee from continuing such breach. Employee affirms having the opportunity to fully discuss and negotiate this Covenant and acknowledges understanding and acceptance. If any part of this Covenant is declared invalid, then Employee agrees to be bound by a Covenant as near to the original as lawfully possible. This paragraph shall survive the term and termination of employment. Employee shall further be liable for all costs of enforcement.

COVENANT 3

Additional Governing Terms

No waiver of a right by Company constitutes a waiver of any other right of Company, and temporary waiver by Company does not constitute a permanent waiver or any additional temporary waiver. These Covenants may be modified only in writing and signed by Employee and Company. If any portion of these Covenants is declared invalid, these Covenants shall continue in effect as if the invalid portion had never been part hereof.

Signed by the Employee   Date

Signed for and on behalf of the Company   Date

[**Warning:** covenants must be drafted according to a particular case and the above is for guidance only.]

EMERGENCY PROCEDURES

The company's emergency procedures in case of crisis are as follows:

Fire: _____

_____

_____

_____

_____

Bomb Threat:_____

_____

_____

_____

_____

Dangerous or threatening person entering the building:_____

_____

_____

_____

_____

Media Crisis: _____

_____

_____

_____

_____

Other:_____

_____

_____

_____

_____

INDEPENDENT CONTRACTOR'S AGREEMENT

THIS AGREEMENT IS MADE the _____ day of _____ year _____

BETWEEN:

(1) _____ (the "Owner"); and

(2) _____ (the "Contractor").

WHEREAS:

(A) The owner resides or operates a business at_____
_____(the "Site") and wishes to have certain services performed at the Site.

(B) The Contractor agrees to perform these services under the terms and conditions set forth in this agreement.

NOW IT IS HEREBY AGREED as follows:

1. **Description of Work**: In return for the payment agreed hereunder the Contractor will perform the following services at the Site:

_____
_____
_____
_____
_____
_____

2. **Payment**: The Owner will pay the Contractor the sum of_____
_____Pounds (£_____) for the work performed under this agreement, under the following schedule:

_____
_____
_____
_____
_____

3. **Relationship of the Parties**: This agreement creates an independent contractor-owner relationship. The Owner is interested only in the results to be achieved. The Contractor is solely responsible for the conduct and control of the work. The Contractor is not an agent

continued on next page

or employee of the Owner for any purpose. Employees of the Contractor are not entitled to any benefits that the Owner provides to the Owner's employees. This is not an exclusive agreement. Both parties are free to contract with other parties for similar services.

4. **Liability:** The Contractor assumes all risk connected with work to be performed. The Contractor also accepts all responsibility for the condition of tools and equipment used in the performance of this agreement and will carry for the duration of this agreement public liability insurance in an amount acceptable to the Owner. The Contractor agrees to indemnify the Owner for any and all liability or loss arising from the performance of this agreement.

5. **Duration:** Either party may cancel this agreement with _____ days' written notice to the other party; otherwise, the contract shall remain in force for a term of _____ _____ from the date hereof.

IN WITNESS OF WHICH the parties have signed this agreement the day and year first above written

_____
Signed by the Owner

_____
in the presence of (witness)

Name _____

Address _____

_____
Occupation _____

_____
Signed by or on behalf of the Contractor

_____
in the presence of (witness)

Name _____

Address _____

_____
Occupation _____

INVENTIONS AND PATENTS AGREEMENT

THIS AGREEMENT IS MADE the _____ day of _____ year _____

BETWEEN:

(1) _____ (the "Employee"); and

(2) _____ (the "Company").

NOW IT IS HEREBY AGREED as follows:

In consideration of the employment of the Employee by the Company, the parties agree as follows:

1. The Employee shall or may have possession of or access to facilities, apparatus, equipment, drawings, systems, formulae, reports, manuals, invention records, customer lists, computer programmes, or other material embodying trade secrets or confidential technical or business information of the Company or its Affiliates. The Employee agrees not to use any such information or material for himself or others, and not to take any such material or reproductions thereof from the Company, at any time during or after employment by the Company, except as required in the Employee's duties to the Company. The Employee agrees immediately to return all such material and reproductions thereof in his possession to the Company upon request and in any event upon termination of employment.

2. Except with prior written authorisation by the Company, the Employee agrees not to disclose or publish any trade secret or confidential technical or business information or material of the Company or its Affiliates or of another party to whom the Company owes an obligation of confidence, at any time during or after employment by the Company.

3. The Employee shall promptly furnish to the Company a complete record of any and all inventions, patents and improvements, whether patentable or not, which he, solely or jointly, may conceive, make, or first disclose during the period of his employment by the Company.

4. The Employee agrees to and hereby grants and assigns to the Company or its nominee the Employee's entire right, title, and interest in and to inventions, patents and improvements that relate in any way to the actual or anticipated business or activities of the Company or its Affiliates, or that are anticipated by or result from any task or work for or on behalf of the Company together with any and all domestic and foreign patent rights in such inventions and improvements. To aid the Company or its nominee in securing full benefit and protection thereof, the Employee agrees promptly to do all lawful acts reasonably requested, at any time during and after employment by the Company, without additional compensation but at the Company's expense.

5. The Employee agrees that, in the event that the Employee accepts employment with any firm or engages in any type of activity on the Employee's own behalf or on behalf of any organisation following termination of his employment with the Company, the Employee shall notify the Company in writing within thirty days of the name and address of such organisation and the nature of such activity.

continued on next page

6. The Employee agrees to give the Company timely written notice of any prior employment agreements or patent rights that might conflict with the interests of the Company or its Affiliates.

7. No waiver by either party of any breach by the other party of any provision of this agreement shall be deemed or construed to be a waiver of any succeeding breach of such provision or as a waiver of the provision itself.

8. This agreement shall be binding upon and pass to the benefit of the successors and assigns of the Company and, insofar as the same may be applied thereto, the heirs, legal representatives, and assigns of the Employee.

9. This agreement shall supersede the terms of any prior employment agreement or understanding between the Employee and the Company. This agreement may be modified or amended only in writing signed by an executive officer of the Company and by the Employee.

10. Should any portion of this agreement be held to be invalid, unenforceable or void, such holding shall not have the effect of invalidating the remainder of this agreement or any other part thereof, the parties hereby agreeing that the portion so held to be invalid, unenforceable, or void shall, if possible, be deemed amended or reduced in scope.

11. The Employee acknowledges reading, understanding and receiving a signed copy of this agreement.

IN WITNESS OF WHICH the parties have signed this agreement the day and year first above written

_____

Signed by the Employer

_____

in the presence of (witness)

Name _____

Address _____

_____

Occupation _____

Signed for and on behalf of the Company

_____

Director

_____

Director/Secretary

NON-COMPETITION AGREEMENT

THIS AGREEMENT IS MADE the _____ day of _____ year _____

BETWEEN:

(1) _____ (the "Company"); and

(2) _____ (the "Employee").

NOW IT IS HEREBY AGREED as follows:

In consideration for the employment of the Employee by the Company the parties agree as follows:

1. The Employee hereby agrees not directly or indirectly to compete with the business of the Company and its successors and assigns during the period of employment and for a period of _____ years following termination of employment and notwithstanding the cause or reason for termination or redundancy.

2. The term "not compete" as used herein shall mean that the Employee shall not own, manage, operate, act as consultant to or be employed in a business substantially similar to or in competition with the present business of the Company or such other business activity in which the Company may substantially engage during the term of employment.

3. The Employee acknowledges that the Company shall or may in reliance of this agreement allow the Employee access to trade secrets, customers and other confidential data and that the provisions of this agreement are reasonably necessary to protect the Company and its goodwill. The Employee agrees to retain this information as confidential and not to use the information on his or her own behalf or disclose the same to any third party.

4. This agreement shall be binding upon and inure to the benefit of the parties, their successors and assigns.

IN WITNESS OF WHICH the parties have signed this agreement the day and year first above written

_____   _____
Signed by the Employee   Signed for and on behalf of the Company

_____   _____
in the presence of (witness)   Director

Name _____

Address _____   _____
                                    Director/Secretary

_____

Occupation _____

[**Warning**: restrictions should only be so wide that they protect the employer's legitimate business interests. Therefore, above agreement is for guidance only and is not 'standard'.]

SALES REPRESENTATIVE AGREEMENT

THIS AGREEMENT is made the _____ day of _____ year _____

BETWEEN:

(1) _____ of _____ (the "Principal"); and

(2) _____ of _____ (the "Representative").

PARTICULARS

This appointment commences on the _____ day of _____ year _____

Sales Territory: _____

Products/Services: _____

Commission Rates: (a)   (subject to (c) below), _____ per cent of the price charged to the customer on all prepaid sales, net of freight, insurance and duties;

    (b)   (subject to (c) below), _____ per cent of the price charged to the customer on all credit sales, net of freight, insurance and duties;

    (c)   a commission percentage to be negotiated between the Principal and the Representative in advance of sale on all orders on which the Principal allows a quantity discount or other trade concession.

Run Off Period: _____ months from the termination of this Agreement.

NOW IT IS HEREBY AGREED as follows:

1. The Representative hereby agrees:

1.1 To represent and sell the Principal's Products/Services in the Sales Territory.

1.2 To represent and state accurately the Principal's policies to all potential and present customers and to make or give no other representations or warranties other than those contained in any standard terms of the Principal.

1.3 To notify promptly all contacts and orders within the Sales Territory, and all enquiries and leads from outside the Sales Territory, to the Principal.

1.4 To inform the Principal or the Principal's sales manager of any problems concerning customers of the Principal within the Sales Territory.

1.5 To inform the Principal or the Principal's sales manager if the Representative is representing, or plans to represent, any other business firm. In no event shall the Representative be involved directly or indirectly with a competing company or product line either within or outside the Sales Territory.

continued on next page

1.6 To provide the Principal upon request with sales reports detailing sales progress within the Sales Territory.

1.7 To return promptly at its expense all materials and samples provided by the Principal to the Representative, if either party terminates this Agreement.

1.8 To indemnify the Principal against any and all loss suffered by the Principal resulting from any breach of this Agreement by the Representative.

2. The Principal agrees:.

2.1 Not later than the last day of the month following the quarter in which the Principal receives payment, to provide the Representative with a statement of commission due, and to pay commission to the Representative at the appropriate Commission Rate on all sales concluded prior to the end of the Run Off Period as a result of, or mainly attributable to, the actions or efforts of the Representative during the appointment.

2.2 To provide the Representative with reasonable quantities of business cards, brochures, catalogues, and product samples required for sales purposes.

3. It is further agreed that:

3.1 Should refunds be made to any customer of the Principal, commission already paid to the Representative on that transaction shall be deducted from future commissions to be paid to the Representative by the Principal.

3.2 Either Party may terminate this Agreement by giving written notice to the other Party. If the Agreement has run for one year or less when notice is served, one month's notice must be given. If it has run for between one and two years, two months' notice must be given. Otherwise, three months' notice must be given unless one Party has committed a material breach in which case the other can terminate without notice.

3.3 The Representative shall have the right to be indemnified as provided in the Commercial Agents (Council Directive) Regulations 1993, but the Representative shall have no right to compensation under those Regulations.

3.4 This constitutes the entire Agreement.

3.5 This Agreement shall be binding upon the Parties and their successors and assigns.

3.6 The Parties are not partners or joint venturers, nor is the Representative able to act as the agent of the Principal except as authorised by this Agreement.

3.7 This Agreement is governed by and shall be construed in accordance with English law.

IN WITNESS OF WHICH the Parties have signed this Agreement the day and year above written

_____   _____

Signed by the Representative   Signed for and on behalf of the Principal

SALES REPRESENTATIVE AGREEMENT: CHANGE IN TERMS

Date _____

To _____

_____

_____

Dear _____

Reference is made to the contract between us dated_____, a copy of which is attached.

This letter will acknowledge that the contract is modified and superseded by the following agreed change in terms:

_____

_____

_____

_____

All other terms shall remain as stated. Unless we immediately hear from you to the contrary, in writing, we shall accept above modification as mutually agreeable, and shall proceed on the modified terms.

Yours sincerely,

_____

Company   The foregoing modification is acknowledged:

_____   _____

By   Sales Representative

SALES REPRESENTATIVE AGREEMENT: EXTENSION

Date _____

To _____

_____

_____

Dear _____

This letter confirms the extension of our agreement made by and between _____ (Sales Representative), and _____ (Company), said Agreement being dated _____ ('the Existing Agreement').

The Existing Agreement expires on, _____, and the parties wish to extend and continue the Existing Agreement for an additional term commencing on the date of expiry of the term contained in the Existing Agreement expiring on _____.

This extension shall be on the same terms and conditions as contained in the original Agreement and as if set forth and incorporated herein excepting only for the following variations to the Existing Agreement which shall take effect from the date of its expiry:

_____

_____

This extension of Agreement shall be binding upon and inure to the benefit of the Sales Representative and the Company and its their successors and assigns.

_____
Company

Acknowledged and Agreed:

_____
By

_____
Sales Representative

_____
Date

[**Note:** the expiry of a fixed-term contract without its renewal has certain implications with regard to the law relating to unfair dismissal and redundancy.]

STAFF HANDBOOK

Table of contents

1. Introduction

This Staff Handbook provides you with a summary of the policies and procedures that operate in the Company. It should be read in conjunction with your contract of employment as both documents form part of your terms and conditions of employment.

To respond to the changing needs of the Company as well as changes in legislation, the policies and procedures may need to be amended from time to time and when this occurs you will be informed of these changes.

If you have any questions about this Staff Handbook please contact your manager.

2. Equal Opportunities Policy

The Company's aim is to ensure that all of its employees and job applicants are treated equally irrespective of disability, race, colour, religion, nationality, ethnic origin, age, sex, sexual orientation or marital status. The Company shall appoint, train, develop and promote on the basis of merit and ability.

All employees have a duty both morally and legally not to discriminate against individuals. This means that there shall be no discrimination on account of disability, race, colour, religion,

continued on next page

- 105 -

nationality, ethnic origin, age, sex, sexual orientation or marital status. Employees have personal responsibility for the practical application of the Company's Equal Opportunities Policy which extends to the treatment of members of the public and employees.

Managers and supervisors who are involved in the recruitment, selection, promotion and training of employees have special responsibility for the practical application of the Company's Equal Opportunities Policy.

The grievance procedure is available to any employee who believes that he or she may have been unfairly discriminated against.

Disciplinary action under the disciplinary procedure shall be taken against any employee who is found to have committed an act of unlawful discrimination. Discriminatory conduct and sexual or racial harassment shall be regarded as gross misconduct.

If there is any doubt about appropriate treatment under the Company's Equal Opportunities Policy, employees should consult their manager.

3. Health & Safety Policy

The Company recognises that it is responsible for ensuring so far as is reasonably practicable the health & safety welfare at work for its employees. The Company believes that pro-active management health and safety issues are an integral part of its obligations to its employees and to the wider community. This policy statement sets out in broad terms the legal responsibilities owed by the Company and by employees in relation to health and safety issues. It will only be possible for the Company to comply with these legal obligations if both its employees and any self-employed third parties on the Company's premises understands that they are under a duty to take reasonable care for the health and safety of themselves and any of their colleagues who may be affected by their acts or omissions and that they are required to cooperate with the Company to enable the Company to perform its obligations.

4. Training

The Company is committed to the continuous development of all its employees. It is vital that employees possess the skills and knowledge to enable them to perform their duties effectively. Any needs should be discussed with the employee's manager on an annual basis. The Company may in its absolute discretion provide financial assistance for external training courses which have relevance to the employees' current or likely future duties with the Company.

5. Business expenses

Employees will be reimbursed for fair and reasonable expenses that are incurred while conducting business on behalf of the Company. Such reimbursement will be made by the Company upon submission of an expense report approved by the employees' manager. Abuse of this right to claim expenses is considered to be gross misconduct which may result in dismissal.

continued on next page

6. Attendance and timekeeping

Employees are expected to attend work punctually at the hours defined in their contract of employment. Employees must receive prior approval from their manager to leave the Company premises during working hours except during lunchbreaks. This will enable the Company to ensure that employees can be located in the event of an emergency.

7. Appearance

Employees are expected to maintain a standard of personal hygiene, appearance and dress appropriate to their job responsibilities.

8. Alcohol

The consumption of alcohol is not allowed on Company premises at any time except where authorised by the employees' manager. No employee should report to work whilst under the influence of alcohol. Breach of this policy may amount to gross misconduct which may result in dismissal.

9. Smoking

Smoking on Company premises is prohibited, apart from designated areas. Employees who do not comply with the no smoking policy, will be subject to disciplinary action.

10. Use of email and the internet

Employees are encouraged to use email and the internet at work as a fast and reliable method of communication with significant advantages for business. However, employees need to be careful not to expose both themselves and the Company to certain risks and offences and that the misuse of these facilities can cause.

Use of external and internal email

- Employees must word all emails appropriately in the same professional manner as if they were composing a letter.

- The content of any email message sent must be neither defamatory, abusive nor illegal and must accord with the Company's Equal Opportunities Policy. Sending and receiving of obscene or pornographic or other offensive material is not only considered to be gross misconduct but may also constitute a criminal offence.

- Employees must be careful of what is said in email messages as the content could give rise to both personal liability or create liability for the Company. Employees must also avoid entering into commitments of themselves or on behalf of the Company over the internet without having received prior and express authorisation to do so or unless this forms part of their normal day-to-day activities and has been so authorised by the Company.

- The Company reserves the right to monitor the content of emails sent and received and may

continued on next page

undertake monitoring of both the content and extent of use of emails. Employees wishing to send confidential non-work related emails should do so on their own equipment in their own time at their own home and should tell personal email contacts never to send any personal emails to them at work.

- Employees must ensure that they have the correct email address for the intended recipients. If employees inadvertently misdirect an email they should contact their manager immediately on becoming aware of their mistake. Failure to do so may lead to disciplinary action being taken against them.

- Employees must not send any information that the Company considers to be confidential or sensitive over the email. The Company, in particular considers the following information inappropriate for transmission over email:

_____

_____

_____

_____

- The email facility is provided for business purposes only. Employees must limit personal usage to a minimum and must abide by the above guidelines concerning the content of emails. Excessive personal usage or abuse of the guidelines concerning the content of emails may lead to the withdrawal of email and internet access and/or disciplinary action which could result in dismissal.

- Employees should at all times remember that email messages may have to be disclosed as evidence at any Court proceedings or investigations by regulatory bodies and therefore may be prejudicial to both their or the Company's interests. Employees should consider that hard copies of emails may be taken and backup discs may retain records of emails even when these have been deleted from the system.

- Disciplinary action under the disciplinary procedure shall be taken against any employee who is found to be in breach of these guidelines and depending upon the circumstances and seriousness of the breach, this may result in summary dismissal.

Using the internet

- Employees must not use the internet to gain unauthorised access or attempt to gain unauthorised access to computer material or private databases.

- Employees must not use the internet for personal purposes whether during work hours or otherwise as this puts an unnecessary strain upon the Company's computer network. Internet access is available purely for business use and it should be used for work related purposes only.

- Internet access may be monitored by the Company and the Company will conduct an audit of internet usage from time to time. Should any breach of these internet guidelines be discovered then employees may, in addition to having internet access being withdrawn, be the

continued on next page

subject of disciplinary action which, in the case of serious breach, may result in dismissal.

- Employees may not subscribe to any news list or groups or commit themselves to receiving information from any group or body without first informing their manager. Employees are requested not to view sites which require the downloading of software from the internet even where this would be free of charge without the prior approval of their manager. Staff are reminded of the risk of computer virus.

- Employees must not attempt to download or retrieve illegal, pornographic, liable, sexist, _ racist, offensive or unlawful material. Attempts to access such material will constitute a disciplinary offence and, in addition to access to the internet being withdrawn, the member of staff may be subject to disciplinary action which may result in dismissal.

- Information on the internet may not have been placed there with the owner's permission. Therefore employees must obtain the permission of the copyright owner before transmitting, copying or downloading such information. Where the copyright owner's consent has clearly been given employees must comply with any terms and conditions stipulated concerning the downloading of such information.

- Information may contain viruses and therefore should not be downloaded from the internet without first obtaining the approval of _____ and/or instructions of _____ concerning the downloading of such information which must be followed. Employees should only download such information that is required for a business purpose. The downloading of information of whatever nature for personal purposes is not permitted.

11. Use of telephones and other facilities

The Company's telephones, mail, faxes and photocopying facilities are provided for business purposes only. Employees must limit personal usage to a minimum. Excessive personal usage may lead to the withdrawal of email and internet access and/or disciplinary action which could result in dismissal.

12. Acceptance of gifts

Employees must not accept directly or indirectly any payment or any other benefit or thing of value of more than nominal value from any supply or customer or from anyone else with any actual or perspective business relationship with the company.

Friendships may develop between customers and employees. However, any relationship between a customer and an employee which is likely to jeopardise business relations in the company is not acceptable. Employees must use their common sense to avoid any actual relationships.

13. Data Protection Policy

Employees may be required to give certain information relating to themselves in order that the Company may properly carry out its duties, rights and obligations as the employer. The Company will process and control such data principally for personnel, administrative and payroll purposes.

continued on next page

The term 'processing' may include the Company obtaining, recording or holding the information or data or carrying out any set of operation or operations on the information or data, including organising, altering, retrieving, consulting, using, disclosing, or destroying the information or data. The Company will adopt appropriate technical and organisational measures to prevent the unauthorised or unlawful processing or disclosure of data.

[It may be necessary to transfer data relating to employees outside of the UK in order that the Company may properly carry out its duties, rights and obligation, in the following circumstances and to the following countries: _____].

Employees are requested to sign the attached consent form giving consent to the Company to process data relating to them which may include sensitive data.

14. Whistleblowing Policy

Employees may, in properly carrying out their duties, have access to, or come into contact with information of a confidential nature. Their terms and conditions provide that except in the proper performance of their duties, employees are forbidden from disclosing or making use of in any form whatsoever such confidential information. However, the law allows employees to make a 'protected disclosure' of certain information. In order to be 'protected' a disclosure must relate to a specific subject matter (listed below) and the disclosure must also be made in an appropriate way.

If in the course of employment, an employee becomes aware of information which they reasonably believe tends to show one or more of the following, they must use the company's disclosure procedure set out below:

- That a criminal offence has been committed, is being committed or is likely to be committed;

- That a person has failed, is failing or is likely to fail to comply with any legal obligation to which he is subject;

- That a miscarriage of justice that has occurred, is occurring, or is likely to occur;

- That the health or safety of any individual has been, is being, or is likely to be, endangered;

- That the environment, has been, is being, or is likely to be, damaged;

- That information tending to show any of the above, is being or is likely to be deliberately concealed.

Disclosure Procedure

Information which an employee reasonably believes tends to show one or more of the above should promptly be disclosed to their manager so that any appropriate action can be taken. If it is inappropriate to make such a disclosure to the manager the employee should speak to _____.

Employees will suffer no detriment of any sort for making such a disclosure in accordance with this procedure. However, failure to follow this procedure may result in the disclosure of information losing its 'protected status'. For further guidance in relation to this matter or concerning the use of

continued on next page

the disclosure procedure generally, employees should speak in confidence to _____.

15. Disciplinary Rules and Procedure

1. The Company's aim is to encourage improvement in individual performance and conduct. Employees are required to treat members of the public and other employees equally in accordance with the Equal Opportunities Policy. This procedure sets out the action which will be taken when disciplinary rules are breached.

2. Principles:

    (i)   The list of rules is not to be regarded as an exhaustive list.

    (ii)   The procedure is designed to establish the facts quickly and to deal consistently with disciplinary issues. No disciplinary action will be taken until the matter has been fully investigated.

    (iii) At every stage employees will have the opportunity to state their case and have a right to be accompanied by a fellow employee or a trade union official of their choice at the hearings.

    (iv)   Only a Director has the right to suspend or dismiss. An employee may, however, be given a verbal or written warning by their immediate superior.

    (v)   An employee has the right to appeal against any disciplinary decision.

3. The Rules:

    Breaches of the Company's disciplinary rules which can lead to disciplinary action are:

    *   failure to observe a reasonable order or instruction;

    *   failure to observe a health and safety requirement;

    *   inadequate time keeping;

    *   absence from work without proper cause (including taking parental leave dishonestly);

    *   theft or removal of the Company's property;

    *   loss, damage to or misuse of the Company's property through negligence or carelessness;

    *   conduct detrimental to the interests of the Company;

    *   incapacity for work due to being under the influence of alcohol or illegal drugs;

    *   physical assault or gross insubordination;

    *   committing an act outside work or being convicted for a criminal offence which is liable adversely to affect the performance of the contract of employment and/or the relationship between the employee and the Company;

continued on next page

- failure to comply with the Company's Equal Opportunities Policy.

4. The Procedure:

(i) *Oral warning*

If conduct or performance is unsatisfactory, the employee will be given a formal oral warning, which will be recorded. The warning will be disregarded after six months' satisfactory service.

(ii) *Written warning*

If the offence is serious, if there is no improvement in standards, or if a further offence occurs, a written warning will be given which will include the reason for the warning and a note that, if there is no improvement after twelve months, a final written warning will be given.

(iii) *Final written warning*

If conduct or performance is still unsatisfactory, or if a further serious offence occurs within the 12-month period, a final written warning will be given making it clear that any recurrence of the offence or other serious misconduct within a period of one month will result in dismissal.

(iv) *Dismissal*

If there is no satisfactory improvement or if further serious misconduct occurs, the employee will be dismissed.

(v) *Gross misconduct*

If, after investigation, it is confirmed that an employee has committed an offence of the following nature (the list is not exhaustive) the normal consequence will be dismissal:

- theft of or damage to the Company's property, incapacity for work due to being under the influence of alcohol or illegal drugs, physical assault and gross insubordination, discrimination or harassment contrary to the Company's Equal Opportunities Policy.

While the alleged gross misconduct is being investigated the employee may be suspended, during which time he or she will be paid the normal hourly rate. Any decision to dismiss will be taken by the employer only after a full investigation.

(vi) *Appeals*

An employee who wishes to appeal against any disciplinary decision must do so to _____ within two working days. The employer will hear the appeal and decide the case as impartially as possible.

16. Grievance Procedure

1. The following procedure shall be applied to settle all disputes or grievances concerning an employee or employees of the Company (but excluding those relating to redundancy selection).

continued on next page

2. Principles:

    (i)   It is the intention of both parties that employees should be encouraged to have direct contact with management to resolve their problems.

    (ii)   The procedure for resolution of grievances and avoidance of disputes is available if the parties are unable to agree a solution to a problem.

    (iii)   Should a matter be referred to this procedure for resolution, both parties should accept that it should be progressed as speedily as possible, with a joint commitment that every effort will be made to ensure that such a reference takes no longer than seven working days to complete.

    (iv)   Pending resolution of the grievance, the same conditions prior to its notification shall continue to apply, except in those circumstances where such a continuation would have damaging effects upon the Company's business.

    (v)   It is agreed between the parties that where the grievance is of a collective nature, i.e. affecting more than one employee, it shall be referred initially to (ii) of the procedure.

    (vi)   If the employee's immediate supervisor/manager is the subject of the grievance and for this reason the employee does not wish the grievance to be heard by him or her, it shall be referred initially to (ii) of the procedure.

3. The Procedure:

    (i)   Where an employee has a grievance, he shall raise the matter with his or her immediate supervisor/manager. If the grievance concerns the performance of a duty by the Company in relation to an employee, the employee shall have a right to be accompanied by a fellow worker or trade union official if they make a request to be so accompanied.

    (ii)   If the matter has not been resolved at (i), it shall be referred to a more senior manager or director and the shop steward, full time trade union officer, or fellow employee, if requested shall be present. A statement summarising the main details of the grievance and the reasons for the failure to agree must be prepared and signed by both parties.

    (iii)   In the event of a failure to agree, the parties will consider whether conciliation or arbitration is appropriate. The Company may refer the dispute to the Advisory Conciliation and Arbitration Service, whose findings may, by mutual prior agreement, be binding on both parties.

I, _____ confirm that I have read and understand this Staff Handbook and accept that it forms part of my terms and conditions of employment.

_____   _____

Signed   Dated

continued on next page

DATA PROTECTION CONSENT FORM

I hereby consent to information relating to me being processed, by the Company in order that it may properly carry out its duties, rights and obligations as my employer. I understand that such processing will principally be for personnel, administrative and payroll purposes.

I understand that information about me shall include information of a sensitive personal nature including information concerning:

[my racial or ethnic origin]

[my political opinions]

[my religious beliefs or other beliefs of a similar nature]

[my membership or non-membership of a Trade Union]

[my physical or mental health or condition]

[my sex life]

[any commission or alleged commission by me of any offence], or

[any proceedings for any offence committed or alleged to have been committed by me, the disposal of such proceedings or the sentence of any court in such proceedings].5

I also understand that the term 'processing' includes the obtaining, recording or holding of information or data or carrying out any operation or set of operations on the information or data, including organising, altering, retrieving, consulting, using, disclosing, combining, or destroying the information or data.

I confirm that I have read and understood this explanation of the processing of data relating to by the Company and that I consent to the processing of such data.

[I consent to the Company transferring the data outside of the UK for the following purposes:

_____

_____

_____

_____]

_____   _____
Signed   Dated

TERMS OF EMPLOYMENT CHANGES

Date _____

To _____

_____

_____

Dear _____

This letter is to let you know that the terms or conditions of your contract have been amended as set out below.

If you wish to discuss any of these changes or require any further information, please let me know.

Date changes effective _____

New wages/salary _____

New hours of work_____

New location _____

Changes to duties and responsibilities _____

Please acknowledge receipt of this letter and your agreement to the terms set out in it by signing the attached copy of this letter and returning it to _____. You should retain the top copy with your contract of employment.

_____

Signed

for_____ Ltd

I, _____, acknowledge that I have received a statement of alteration to the particulars of my employment as required by the Employment Rights Act 1996 Section 1 and agree to the terms set out in that statement.

_____   _____

Signed   Date

TERMS OF EMPLOYMENT SUMMARY

Date _____

To _____

_____

_____

Dear _____

We are pleased you have accepted a position with our company, and want to take this opportunity to summarise your initial terms and conditions of employment.

1. Commencement date of employment: _____

2. Position/title: _____

3. Starting salary: _____

4. Weeks holiday/year: _____

5. Eligible for holiday starting: _____

6. Health insurance: _____

_____

7. Pension/Profit-Sharing: _____

_____

8. Other benefits: _____

_____

9. Other terms/conditions: _____

_____

If this is not in accordance with your understanding, please let me know immediately. We look forward to you joining us.

Yours sincerely,

_____

DIRECT DEPOSIT AUTHORISATION

Employee:_____

Dept./Position:_____ Identification No.: _____

Bank Name and Branch:_____

Sort Code:_____Account No.: _____

Tick appropriate box:

[   ] I hereby request the deposit of my entire net salary into the above-named bank account each pay period. I authorise _____ and for _____to withdraw any funds deposited in error into my account.

[   ] I hereby request and authorise the sum of _____ pounds (£   ) to be deducted from my salary each pay period and be deposited directly into the bank account named above.

[   ] I hereby cancel the authorisation for direct deposit or payroll deduction deposit previously submitted.

_____
Employee

_____
Date

Please attach copy of deposit slip.

PAY ADVICE

_____ Ltd.

Name: _____   Date: _____

Works/Dept No.: _____   Tax Code: _____

National Insurance: _____   Tax Week: _____

Payments	Hours	Rate £	p	Total £	p
Basic	_____				
Overtime	_____				
Bonus, holiday, sick pay	_____				
Gross payable					

Deductions	£	p
Company Pension		
Income tax		
National Insurance		
Standard rate at _____%		
Reduced rate at _____%		
Other deductions		
Total deductions		
Net payable		

Keep this as a record of your earnings

PAY OR GRADE CHANGE FOLLOWING JOB EVALUATION

Date _____

To _____

_____

_____

Dear _____

Following our job evaluation review it has been decided to upgrade your job title to _____ with effect from _____.

From that date your salary will be increased to £ _____ per _____. All other terms and conditions of your employment remain unchanged.

We offer our congratulations on your promotion, and hope that you enjoy your new position.

Yours sincerely,

_____

PAYROLL CHANGE NOTICE

Date: _____   Effective Date: _____

_____ Enter on payroll	_____ Promotion
_____ Change rate	_____ Discharged
_____ Transfer to _____	_____ Temp. _____
_____ Layoff	
_____ Redundancy	
_____ Remove from Payroll	_____ Raise
_____ Resignation	
_____ Dismissed	

Employee _____

Employee number _____

Old rate _____

New rate _____

Comments _____

_____

_____   _____
Submitted By   Date

_____   _____
Approved By   Date

PAYROLL FOR DEPARTMENT

Period beginning: _____ Ending: _____

| Employee | Hours | | Pay | Wages | | Total |
	Reg	OT	Rate	Reg	OT	Wages
_____	_____	_____	_____	_____	_____	_____
_____	_____	_____	_____	_____	_____	_____
_____	_____	_____	_____	_____	_____	_____
_____	_____	_____	_____	_____	_____	_____
_____	_____	_____	_____	_____	_____	_____
_____	_____	_____	_____	_____	_____	_____
_____	_____	_____	_____	_____	_____	_____
_____	_____	_____	_____	_____	_____	_____
_____	_____	_____	_____	_____	_____	_____
_____	_____	_____	_____	_____	_____	_____
_____	_____	_____	_____	_____	_____	_____
_____	_____	_____	_____	_____	_____	_____
_____	_____	_____	_____	_____	_____	_____
_____	_____	_____	_____	_____	_____	_____
_____	_____	_____	_____	_____	_____	_____
_____	_____	_____	_____	_____	_____	_____
_____	_____	_____	_____	_____	_____	_____
_____	_____	_____	_____	_____	_____	_____
_____	_____	_____	_____	_____	_____	_____
_____	_____	_____	_____	_____	_____	_____
Totals:	_____	_____	_____	_____	_____	_____

SALARY CHANGE REQUEST

Employee: _____ Date Started: _____

Department: _____ Supervisor: _____

Position(s): _____

Last Two Increases

(1) From £_____ to £_____   Date _____

(2) From £_____ to £_____   Date _____

Last Performance Analysis: _____

(   ) **Salary increase recommended**

From £_____ to £_____   Effective _____

_____ Merit   _____ In Budget   _____ Exempt

_____ Adjustment   _____ Not in Budget   _____ Non-Exempt

_____ Promotion (If promotion, attach new job description.)

Reason for increase: _____

_____

(   ) **No salary increase recommended**

Based on performance analysis dated: _____

Other:_____

_____

Comments:_____

_____

_____

_____

_____   _____

Signed   Date

SALARY DEDUCTION AUTHORISATION

The undersigned hereby authorises _____

to deduct £_____ from my earnings each payroll period, beginning on _____,

for the following:

In payment for: Amount

_____   Pension Scheme   _____

_____   Medical Insurance   _____

_____   Union Subscription etc   _____

_____   _____   _____

_____   _____   _____

_____   _____   _____

_____   _____   _____

                                     Total £ _____

_____   _____

Signature   Date

Print Name: _____

Department/Position: _____

Please retain a copy of this for your records.

SALARY DEDUCTION DIRECT DEPOSIT AUTHORISATION

Name: _____ Department.: _____

Position: _____ Identification No.: _____

Bank Name & Branch: _____

Sort Code:_____Account No.: _____

Tick appropriate box:

[   ] Direct payroll deduction

The undersigned hereby requests and authorises the sum of _____
_____ pounds (£   ) be deducted from my net salary each
pay period and to be deposited directly into the bank account named above.

[   ] Cancellation of deposit authorisation:

The undersigned hereby cancels the authorisation for direct deposit previously submitted.

_____
Employee

_____
Date

Please attach copy of deposit slip.

SALARY RECORD

Employee: _____

Starting date: _____ Starting salary: _____

Position	Increase date	Increase	Type of increase (merit/promotion/ etc.)
_____	_____	_____	_____
_____	_____	_____	_____
_____	_____	_____	_____
_____	_____	_____	_____
_____	_____	_____	_____
_____	_____	_____	_____
_____	_____	_____	_____
_____	_____	_____	_____
_____	_____	_____	_____
_____	_____	_____	_____
_____	_____	_____	_____
_____	_____	_____	_____
_____	_____	_____	_____
_____	_____	_____	_____
_____	_____	_____	_____
_____	_____	_____	_____
_____	_____	_____	_____
_____	_____	_____	_____
_____	_____	_____	_____

SALARY RISE: LETTER TO EMPLOYEE

Date _____

To _____

_____

_____

Dear _____

It is with pleasure that I write to let you know of our decision to increase your salary. The increase is £ _____ per _____ .

This increase is only partly in recognition of the increase in the cost of living since your last rise. It is also made in reward for your loyal and conscientious work, and to let you know that your efforts have been recognised. The increase will take effect from the beginning of this month.

I hope that we shall be able to continue our happy working relationship for many years to come.

Yours sincerely,

_____

FLEXITIME SCHEDULE

Employee:_____ Week Ending: _____

Day	Time In	Time Out	Hours/Day
Monday	_____	_____	_____
Tuesday	_____	_____	_____
Wednesday	_____	_____	_____
Thursday	_____	_____	_____
Friday	_____	_____	_____
Saturday	_____	_____	_____
Sunday	_____	_____	_____

Weekly Total: _____

NIGHT WORK ACCEPTANCE AGREEMENT

A second shift is or may be required to meet our present or future needs. All new employees are hired on the understanding that they are able and willing to work night shifts.

Please answer the following:

		YES	NO
1.	Do you have any physical disability that would prevent you from working night shifts?	_____	_____
2.	Do you know of any personal reasons that would interfere with your working night shifts?	_____	_____
3.	Are you willing to work night shifts?	_____	_____

I understand that any employment is conditional upon my acceptance of a night assignment if required.

_____
Signed

_____
Date

_____
Witness

In case of emergency notify:

Name _____   Tel _____

Address _____   Relationship _____

_____

Name _____   Tel _____

Address _____   Relationship _____

_____

[**Note:** there are certain obligations that employers must comply with under the Working Time Regulations 1998 when engaging night workers.]

OVERTIME AUTHORISATION

Department:_____ Date: _____

Employee: _____ Employee ID No.:_____

Overtime Hours Authorised: _____

Reason for Overtime: _____

_____

_____

_____

_____

_____

_____

_____

_____

_____

_____

_____

_____

Requested by: _____

Title: _____ Date: _____

Approved by: _____

Title: _____ Date: _____

OVERTIME REPORT: INDIVIDUAL

Department:_____ Date: _____

Payroll Period	Total Hours	Total Salaries	% of Payroll
_____	_____	_____	_____
_____	_____	_____	_____
_____	_____	_____	_____
_____	_____	_____	_____
_____	_____	_____	_____
_____	_____	_____	_____
_____	_____	_____	_____
_____	_____	_____	_____
_____	_____	_____	_____
_____	_____	_____	_____
_____	_____	_____	_____
_____	_____	_____	_____
_____	_____	_____	_____
_____	_____	_____	_____
_____	_____	_____	_____
_____	_____	_____	_____
_____	_____	_____	_____

_____   _____
Approval Requested By   Date

_____   _____
Approved By   Date

OVERTIME REPORT: DEPARTMENTAL

Department: _____ Time Period: _____

Supervisor: _____

Employee	Date	Overtime Hours	Overtime Paid	% of Payroll
_____	_____	_____	_____	_____
_____	_____	_____	_____	_____
_____	_____	_____	_____	_____
_____	_____	_____	_____	_____
_____	_____	_____	_____	_____
_____	_____	_____	_____	_____
_____	_____	_____	_____	_____
_____	_____	_____	_____	_____
_____	_____	_____	_____	_____
_____	_____	_____	_____	_____
_____	_____	_____	_____	_____
_____	_____	_____	_____	_____
_____	_____	_____	_____	_____
_____	_____	_____	_____	_____
_____	_____	_____	_____	_____
_____	_____	_____	_____	_____

_____   _____
Submitted By   Date

_____   _____
Approved By   Date

OVERTIME REQUEST: DEPARTMENTAL

Department: _____ Date: _____

Employee	Employee ID No.	Overtime Requested	Authorised
_____	_____	_____	_____
_____	_____	_____	_____
_____	_____	_____	_____
_____	_____	_____	_____
_____	_____	_____	_____
_____	_____	_____	_____
_____	_____	_____	_____
_____	_____	_____	_____
_____	_____	_____	_____
_____	_____	_____	_____
_____	_____	_____	_____
_____	_____	_____	_____
_____	_____	_____	_____
_____	_____	_____	_____
_____	_____	_____	_____
_____	_____	_____	_____

Total: _____

Signature: _____

TIME RECORD: DAILY 1

Day: _____ Date: _____

Employee	Time Began	Time Ended	Overtime	Comments
_____	_____	_____	_____	_____
_____	_____	_____	_____	_____
_____	_____	_____	_____	_____
_____	_____	_____	_____	_____
_____	_____	_____	_____	_____
_____	_____	_____	_____	_____
_____	_____	_____	_____	_____
_____	_____	_____	_____	_____
_____	_____	_____	_____	_____
_____	_____	_____	_____	_____
_____	_____	_____	_____	_____
_____	_____	_____	_____	_____
_____	_____	_____	_____	_____
_____	_____	_____	_____	_____
_____	_____	_____	_____	_____
_____	_____	_____	_____	_____
_____	_____	_____	_____	_____
_____	_____	_____	_____	_____
_____	_____	_____	_____	_____
_____	_____	_____	_____	_____
_____	_____	_____	_____	_____
_____	_____	_____	_____	_____
_____	_____	_____	_____	_____
_____	_____	_____	_____	_____
_____	_____	_____	_____	_____
_____	_____	_____	_____	_____
_____	_____	_____	_____	_____

By: _____

TIME RECORD: DAILY 2

Employee: _____ Period Ending: _____

Department: _____ Supervisor: _____

Date	Time Started	Time Finished	Overtime	Total
_____	_____	_____	_____	_____
_____	_____	_____	_____	_____
_____	_____	_____	_____	_____
_____	_____	_____	_____	_____
_____	_____	_____	_____	_____
_____	_____	_____	_____	_____
_____	_____	_____	_____	_____
_____	_____	_____	_____	_____
_____	_____	_____	_____	_____
_____	_____	_____	_____	_____
_____	_____	_____	_____	_____
_____	_____	_____	_____	_____
_____	_____	_____	_____	_____
_____	_____	_____	_____	_____
_____	_____	_____	_____	_____

By: _____ Title: _____ Date: _____

TIME SHEET: WEEKLY

Complete hours for each employee and for each day worked. Mark days not worked.

Week of: _____ year _____ .

Employee	Sun	Mon	Tue	Wed	Thu	Fri	Sat	Total
_____	___	___	___	___	___	___	___	___
_____	___	___	___	___	___	___	___	___
_____	___	___	___	___	___	___	___	___
_____	___	___	___	___	___	___	___	___
_____	___	___	___	___	___	___	___	___
_____	___	___	___	___	___	___	___	___
_____	___	___	___	___	___	___	___	___
_____	___	___	___	___	___	___	___	___
_____	___	___	___	___	___	___	___	___
_____	___	___	___	___	___	___	___	___
_____	___	___	___	___	___	___	___	___
_____	___	___	___	___	___	___	___	___
_____	___	___	___	___	___	___	___	___
_____	___	___	___	___	___	___	___	___
_____	___	___	___	___	___	___	___	___
_____	___	___	___	___	___	___	___	___
_____	___	___	___	___	___	___	___	___
_____	___	___	___	___	___	___	___	___
_____	___	___	___	___	___	___	___	___
Totals:	___	___	___	___	___	___	___	___

WORK SCHEDULE WEEKLY

Week Ending: _____

HOURS

Employee	Sun	Mon	Tue	Wed	Thu	Fri	Sat
_____	____	____	____	____	____	____	____
_____	____	____	____	____	____	____	____
_____	____	____	____	____	____	____	____
_____	____	____	____	____	____	____	____
_____	____	____	____	____	____	____	____
_____	____	____	____	____	____	____	____
_____	____	____	____	____	____	____	____
_____	____	____	____	____	____	____	____
_____	____	____	____	____	____	____	____
_____	____	____	____	____	____	____	____
_____	____	____	____	____	____	____	____
_____	____	____	____	____	____	____	____
_____	____	____	____	____	____	____	____
_____	____	____	____	____	____	____	____
_____	____	____	____	____	____	____	____
_____	____	____	____	____	____	____	____
_____	____	____	____	____	____	____	____
_____	____	____	____	____	____	____	____
_____	____	____	____	____	____	____	____
_____	____	____	____	____	____	____	____
_____	____	____	____	____	____	____	____

WORKING TIME REGULATIONS OPT OUT AGREEMENT

Date _____

To _____

_____

_____

Dear _____

On 1st October 1998 the Working Time Regulations 1998 placed restrictions on the average number of hours an individual employee is able to work per week.

The problem: The regulations clearly state that employees must not work more than an average of 48 hours per week. This 48-hour average includes both basic working time and any overtime. Therefore, the law means that you are prevented from working any overtime which would result in your average working week exceeding 48 hours.

The solution: The Regulations enable individual employees to 'opt out' and work in excess of this 48-hour limit. However, any agreement to opt out of this 48-hour limit must be in writing. Therefore, the Company would be grateful if you would sign and date the Consent Form enclosed and return it to _____ before _____.

If you sign the Consent Form, this arrangement is not necessarily permanent. Should you decide that you no longer wish to opt out of the 48-hour maximum working week, then you can withdraw your consent by giving the Company three months' written notice of this intention.

Refusal to sign the Consent Form will not result in any disciplinary or other action against you. However, it will mean that you are prevented from working any overtime which would result in your average working week exceeding 48 hours.

If you have any queries in relation to any aspect of this letter, please do not hesitate to contact _____. We look forward to hearing from you.

Yours sincerely,

_____

continued on next page

INDIVIDUAL AGREEMENT
(pursuant to Regulation 5 of the Working Time Directive 1998 no 1833)

I hereby agree:

1.   that Regulation 4(1) of the Working Time Regulations 1998 will not apply in relation to my working hours [providing that ... *insert any specific conditions that the employee requires which amount to provisos of his/her agreement to disapply Regulation 4(1)*].

2.   to work in excess of 48 hours per week on average if reasonably necessary pursuant to the obligations under my contract of employment; and

3.   to provide the Company with three months' notice in writing of my intention to terminate this agreement.

Signed

_____ (Signature of employee)

Date

_____

Section 4
Employment Benefits & Leave

Expenses & Benefits:

Accrued Benefits Statement – Lists type and amount of benefits accrued by specific employee.

Benefits Analysis – Adds company and employee contribution to a given benefit to determine the total annual cost of the benefit.

Benefits List – Outlines benefits offered employees.

Benefits Planning Checklist – Compares current company benefits with competitor's policy and employee's preferences, and makes a recommendation.

Benefits Survey – Seeks employees' opinions of current company benefits.

Expenses Recovery Agreement – Employee agrees to repay company for any disallowed expense deductions for which employee was reimbursed.

Expenses Report - Records an employee's expenses for a company trip.

Mileage Reimbursement Report - Records an employee's company reimbursable mileage for a given month.

Relocation Expense Approval – Authorises payment of new employee's relocation expenses.

Paid & Unpaid Leave:

Absence Report 1 - Department report of employees' absences.

Absence Report 2 - Record of employee's absence.

Absence Report 3 - Supervisor's report of employee's absence.

Absence Request - Employee's request to miss work.

Absent Believed Sick Letter to Employee - A letter to employee on extended absence.

Accident Report - Records events of an accident.

Disability Certificate - Certifies an employee's disability.

Doctor's Report - Certifies that an employee's absence is medically necessary.

Funeral Leave Request - Employee's request to miss work for a funeral.

Holiday Request - Records an employee's requested holiday dates.

Holiday Request Memo - Employee's request to take a specified number of holiday days.

Illness Report - Records an employee's illness that affects employment.

Injury Report - Records an employee's injury.

Leave/Return from Leave Request - Record of employee's reason for absence.

Maternity Absent Employee's Letter to Employer regarding Return to Work - A letter from an employee stating intention to return to work.

Maternity Leave and Maternity Absence Request to Employer - A letter from an employee giving notice of her intention to take maternity leave and maternity absence until the 28th week after the week of childbirth.

Maternity Leave Employee intending to Take Maternity Absence: Letter from Employer - A letter asking an employee about her intentions to return to work after maternity absence.

Maternity Leave Request to Employer - A letter from an employee giving notice of her intention to take maternity leave.

Sympathy Letter 1 - Letter to injured employee.

Sympathy Letter 2 - Letter to ill employee.

Sympathy Letter 3 - Letter to injured employee.

Sympathy Letter 4 - Letter to ill employee.

ACCRUED BENEFITS STATEMENT

Employee:_____

Department: _____ Benefits accrued to (date):_____

Accrued Holiday Days: _____

Accrued Holiday Pay: £_____

Accrued Sick Days: _____

Accrued Sick Pay: £_____

Share Dividends: £_____

Company Shares: _____

Severance Pay: £_____

Accrued Reimbursable Expenses: £_____

Other Benefits:

_____   _____

_____   _____

_____   _____

This is an _____ interim _____ final statement.

This statement is subject to corrections.

_____   _____

Signed   Date

BENEFITS ANALYSIS

	Company Contribution	Employee Contribution	Benefit Total Cost (Annual)
Share Option :	£_____	£_____	£_____
Medical Insurance:	£_____	£_____	£_____
Group Life Insurance:	£_____	£_____	£_____
Subsidised mortgage:	£_____	£_____	£_____
Low-Interest Loans:	£_____	£_____	£_____
Education sponsorship	£_____	£_____	£_____
Profit-Sharing:	£_____	£_____	£_____
Performance Bonus:	£_____	£_____	£_____
Relocation Expenses:	£_____	£_____	£_____
Company Pension:	£_____	£_____	£_____
Child Care:	£_____	£_____	£_____
Club Memberships:	£_____	£_____	£_____
Mobile phone:	£_____	£_____	£_____
Home telephone:	£_____	£_____	£_____
Lap-top computer:	£_____	£_____	£_____
Company Car:	£_____	£_____	£_____
Financial Counselling:	£_____	£_____	£_____
Sabbaticals:	£_____	£_____	£_____
Entertainment:	£_____	£_____	£_____
Work dress/uniform:	£_____	£_____	£_____
Other:	£_____	£_____	£_____

BENEFITS LIST

A. Group Life Insurance

_____

_____

_____

B. Medical Insurance

_____

_____

_____

_____

C. Pension Plan

_____

_____

_____

D. Profit-Sharing Plan

_____

_____

_____

E. Employee Share Purchase Plan

_____

_____

_____

F. Other

_____

_____

_____

BENEFITS PLANNING CHECKLIST

	Company Policy	Competitor Policy	Employee Preference	Recommendation
Incentive Share Option:	_____	_____	_____	_____
Medical Insurance:	_____	_____	_____	_____
Group Life Insurance:	_____	_____	_____	_____
Education Benefits:	_____	_____	_____	_____
Profit-Sharing:	_____	_____	_____	_____
Performance Bonus:	_____	_____	_____	_____
Education sponsorship:	_____	_____	_____	_____
Relocation Expenses:	_____	_____	_____	_____
Pension:	_____	_____	_____	_____
Financial Counselling:	_____	_____	_____	_____
Child Care:	_____	_____	_____	_____
Club Memberships:	_____	_____	_____	_____
Share Option Scheme:	_____	_____	_____	_____
Low-Interest Loans:	_____	_____	_____	_____
Mobile phone:	_____	_____	_____	_____
Lap-top computer:	_____	_____	_____	_____
Home telephone:	_____	_____	_____	_____
Company Car:	_____	_____	_____	_____
Sabbaticals:	_____	_____	_____	_____
Entertainment:	_____	_____	_____	_____
Work dress/uniform:	_____	_____	_____	_____
Other:	_____	_____	_____	_____

BENEFITS SURVEY

We want your opinion on the importance of each employee benefit presently offered, as well as other benefits under consideration. Please rank each benefit listed in order of relative interest to you. Use a 1-10 scale, 1 meaning top priority and 10 indicating the lowest. You comments are also invited.

Benefit	Priority	Comments
Incentive Share Option:	_____	_____
Health Insurance:	_____	_____
Group Life Insurance:	_____	_____
Education Sponsorship:	_____	_____
Profit-Sharing:	_____	_____
Performance Bonus:	_____	_____
Relocation Expenses:	_____	_____
Company Pension	_____	_____
Child Care:	_____	_____
Club Memberships:	_____	_____
Low-Interest Loans:	_____	_____
Mobile phone:	_____	_____
Home telephone:	_____	_____
Lap-top computer:	_____	_____
Company Car:	_____	_____
Financial Counselling:	_____	_____
Sabbaticals:	_____	_____
Work dress/uniform:	_____	_____
Entertainment:	_____	_____
Other: _____	_____	_____

EXPENSES RECOVERY AGREEMENT

To_____

_____

_____

In consideration of the Employer agreeing to reimburse the Employee's expenses incurred in connection with his employment the undersigned Employee of _____ (Employer) hereby agrees to repay to Employer all amounts paid by the Employer to the Employee as compensation for or reimbursement of expenses incurred in the course of employment for which, in the Employer's reasonable opinion, no substantiating or insufficient substantiating evidence has been provided. The Employer may reimburse itself for such amounts by deducting them from salary and other cash benefits due to the Employee.

In the presence of:

_____   _____
Employee   Date

_____   _____
Witness   Date

EXPENSES REPORT

EXPENSE CLAIM FORM

CLAIMANT: MONTH

DATE	RECEIPT NUMBER	EXPENSE	TOTAL	VAT	FUEL/ MILEAGE	CAR EXPENSES	SUBSIST/ UK TRAVEL	OVERSEAS TRAVEL	ENTERTAINMENT CLIENT	ENTERTAINMENT STAFF	PHONE	OFFICE SUPPLIES	SUNDRIES
	1												
	2												
	3												
	4												
	5												
	6												
	7												
	8												
	9												
	10												
	11												
	12												
	13												
	14												
	15												
	16												
	17												
	18												
	19												
	20												
	21												
	22												
	23												
SUB TOTAL			£	£	£	£	£	£	£	£	£	£	£

TOTAL CLAIMED   £

SIGNATURE: APPROVED:

MILEAGE REIMBURSEMENT REPORT

Employee: _____

Driver's License No.: _____ Insurance No.: _____

Type of Vehicle: _____

Department: _____ Month: _____

Date	Beginning Reading	Ending Reading	Total Mileage	Reason for Travel
_____	_____	_____	_____	_____
_____	_____	_____	_____	_____
_____	_____	_____	_____	_____
_____	_____	_____	_____	_____
_____	_____	_____	_____	_____
_____	_____	_____	_____	_____
_____	_____	_____	_____	_____
_____	_____	_____	_____	_____
_____	_____	_____	_____	_____
_____	_____	_____	_____	_____
_____	_____	_____	_____	_____
_____	_____	_____	_____	_____
_____	_____	_____	_____	_____
_____	_____	_____	_____	_____

Total mileage this month: _____ @ £ 0._____ Per Mile = £_____

_____   _____

Approved By   Date

Title: _____

RELOCATION EXPENSE APPROVAL

Employee name: _____

Account to be charged: _____ Position: _____

Prior location: _____ New location: _____

Effective date of employment: _____ Present home: Own _____ Rented _____

Married _____ Single _____ No. of Dependents _____

	Estimated Cost	Actual Cost
1. Cost of moving household goods	£_____	£ _____
2. Employee travel and lodging to new location	£_____	£ _____
3. Family travel and lodging to new location	£_____	£ _____
4. House-hunting travel and lodging for employee up to 4 days	£_____	£ _____
5. Incidental expense allowance of _____ month's salary	£_____	£ _____
7. Other special items (specify)	£_____	£ _____
_____	£_____	£ _____
_____	£_____	£ _____
_____	£_____	£ _____
TOTAL:	£_____	£ _____

Employee's Signature _____ Date _____

Approvals:

Department Manager _____ Date _____

Managing Director _____ Date _____

ABSENCE REPORT 1

Department:_____ Date: _____

The following employees were absent from work today:

Employee	Reason for absence	Paid/ Unpaid
_____	_____	_____
_____	_____	_____
_____	_____	_____
_____	_____	_____
_____	_____	_____
_____	_____	_____
_____	_____	_____
_____	_____	_____
_____	_____	_____
_____	_____	_____
_____	_____	_____
_____	_____	_____
_____	_____	_____
_____	_____	_____
_____	_____	_____
_____	_____	_____
_____	_____	_____

_____
Signed

ABSENCE REPORT 2

Employee: _____ Date: _____

Report received by: _____

Expected No. of days absent: _____ Expected date of return: _____

Time of report: _____

Absence reported to: _____

Reported by   (   ) Self   (   ) Other relative

                (   ) Spouse   (   ) Friend

                (   ) Supervisor (   ) Other: _____

Reason

                (   ) Illness   (   ) Illness in family

                (   ) Injury on job (   ) Outside injury

                (   ) Travel   (   ) Death in family

                (   ) Jury service

                (   ) Other: _____

_____

_____

_____

_____
Signed

Comments: _____

_____

_____

_____

_____

_____

ABSENCE REPORT 3

Employee: _____ Date: _____

Department: _____

Date(s) Absent: _____ Date of Return: _____ Day(s) Missed: _____

Did employee notify company in advance?   Yes (   )   No (   )

Reason for Absence: _____

_____

_____

Was Absence Approved?   Yes (   )   No (   )

Reason for Non-Notification: _____

_____

_____

Action Taken:

_____   None

_____   Deduct Pay

_____   Make up time

_____   Warning

_____   Dismiss

_____   Other: _____

Comments: _____

_____

_____

_____

_____   _____
Signed   Date

Title: _____

ABSENCE REQUEST

Employee: _____ Date: _____

Department: _____

Date(s) Requested: From: _____ to_____

Hours Requested: From: _____ to_____

With Pay (   )   Without Pay (   )   Makeup (   )

Reason for Absence: _____

_____

_____

_____

_____

_____

_____

_____

_____

         Approved (   )   Not Approved (   )

Supervisor Comments: _____

_____

_____

_____

_____

_____   _____
Employee   Date

_____   _____
Supervisor   Date

ABSENT BELIEVED SICK LETTER TO EMPLOYEE

Date _____

To _____

_____

_____

Dear _____

You have not been to work since _____ , and have failed to contact me to let me know why.

Please let me know at once the reason for your absence from work and, if you are unwell, provide me with a certificate from your doctor. Without this certificate, you are not entitled to any sick pay.

In case you do not know about the sickness regulations, you are only entitled to statutory sick pay for the first 28 weeks of your absence through sickness. After that you must claim state benefit.

Yours sincerely,

_____

ACCIDENT REPORT

Employee: _____ Age: _____ Sex: _____

Department:_____ Supervisor: _____

Date of accident: _____

Nature of injuries:_____

_____

_____

Cause of Accident: _____

_____

_____

If employee left work, time of leaving: _____

If employee returned to work, time of return: _____

Name and address of doctor: _____

_____

If hospitalised, name and address of hospital: _____

_____

Actions undertaken to avoid similar incidents: _____

_____

_____

Comments:_____

_____

_____

_____

_____   _____
Supervisor   Date

DISABILITY CERTIFICATE

To be completed by employee:

Employee:_____

_____

Address: _____

_____ Phone: _____

I authorise Dr _____ to release necessary information to the company referred
to below regarding my condition while under his/her care.

_____   _____
Employee's Signature   Date

To be completed by attending doctor:

Date disability began:_____

Expected return to work date: _____

Nature of disability: _____

_____

Special complications:_____

Work restrictions: _____

_____

Date(s) seen: _____

If hospitalised, name of hospital: _____

Dates: From _____ to _____

Date of surgery, if any:_____ Procedure:_____

If pregnancy, expected date of delivery:_____

Doctor's name: _____

_____   _____
Doctor's signature   Date
Address: _____

_____ Phone: _____

Return to: (Company)   _____

_____

_____

- 156 -

DOCTOR'S REPORT

Date _____

To Dr _____

Re _____

Dear Doctor _____

The above named employee has been absent from work from _____
to _____ and we have been advised that our employee has
been under your medical care.

Since we verify protracted medical-related absences, we would appreciate your completing this
form and returning it for our records.

Yours sincerely

_____

Doctor's Report

_____
_____
_____
_____

I certify that _____ has been
under my _____ medical care
and that the absences listed above were medically necessary or reasonable based on the medical
condition.

_____   _____
Doctor   Date

- 157 -

FUNERAL LEAVE REQUEST

Employee: _____ Date: _____

Department: _____

Dates of missed work days: _____ Hourly Rate: _____

Name of Deceased: _____ Funeral Date: _____

Residence (town): _____ Country: _____

Burial Place: _____

Relationship to employee: _____

_____

_____

Comments: _____

_____

_____

_____
Employee

Approved

_____
Supervisor

HOLIDAY REQUEST

Employee: _____ Employment Date: _____

I request a _____ week holiday:

From _____ to _____

My alternative choice is:

From: _____ to _____

(if a Bank holiday occurs during your holiday, please request extra days below.)

_____

_____

_____

I prefer to split my holiday:

    First Week: From:_____ to _____

    Second Week: From:_____ to _____

    Third Week: From:_____ to _____

    Fourth Week: From:_____ to _____

Below holiday dates approved by: _____

Date: _____

Approved holiday dates: _____

HOLIDAY REQUEST MEMO

MEMO TO: Payroll Department

I request permission to take_____ days' holiday from_____
to_____. These days have not yet accrued and I agree that
if I leave the Company before this holiday time or any of it has accrued, the Company may deduct
the equivalent number of days' earnings from my final salary cheque in compensation.

_____   _____
Employee   Date

_____   _____
Supervisor   Date

ILLNESS REPORT

Employee: _____ Date: _____

Age: _____ Sex: _____

Department: _____ Supervisor: _____

Is illness related to employment?   Yes (   )   No (   )

Date of diagnosis: _____

Describe illness:

_____

_____

_____

If employee left work, time of leaving: _____

If employee returned to work, time of return: _____

Name and address of doctor: _____

_____

If hospitalised, name and address of hospital: _____

_____

Comments: _____

_____

_____

_____

_____

_____

_____   _____
Supervisor   Date

INJURY REPORT

Name: _____ National Insurance No:_____

Address: _____

_____ Phone: _____

Age: _____ Sex: _____

Is injury related to employment?   Yes (   ) No (   )

Describe:_____

Date of injury: _____ Time of injury: _____

Date of initial diagnosis:_____

Describe the injury in detail and indicate the part of the body affected:

_____

Did employee return to work? Yes (   ) No (   ) If no, indicate last day worked:

_____

Name and address of doctor: _____

_____

If hospitalised, name and address of hospital: _____

_____

Names of witnesses: _____

_____

Comments:_____

_____

_____

_____   _____
Employee   Date

_____   _____
Supervisor or first aid person   Date

LEAVE/RETURN FROM LEAVE REQUEST

Employee: _____ Date: _____

Position: _____ Date Employed: _____

Leave Request

Reason for Leave:

_____ Personal Disability

_____ Training Conference

_____ Compensatory Time Off

_____ Jury Service

_____ Family Illness (Name) _____

_____ Family Death (Name) _____

_____ Other (Explain) _____

_____ _____

_____ _____

Leave Requested:

From: Date:_____ Time: _____ Total Hours: _____

To: Date: _____ Time: _____ Total Days: _____

Regular work schedule: _____

_____   _____

Employee   Date

Return From Leave

Absent from: Date: _____ Time:_____ Total Hours: _____

To: Date: _____ Time:_____ Total Days: _____

_____ Excused/Warranted

_____ Not Excused/Not Warranted (Explain) _____

_____ Resumed Part-Time Work

_____ Resumed Full-Time Work

_____ Resumed Modified Duty (Explain) _____

_____ Other (Explain) _____

Affirmed By: _____ Date: _____

MATERNITY ABSENT EMPLOYEE'S LETTER TO EMPLOYER REGARDING RETURN TO WORK

Date _____

To _____
_____
_____

Dear _____

As required, I am writing to you at least 21 days before I exercise my right to return to work.

I intend to return to work on _____.

Yours sincerely,

_____

MATERNITY LEAVE AND MATERNITY ABSENCE REQUEST TO EMPLOYER

Date _____

To _____

_____

_____

Dear _____

This is to inform you that I am pregnant and wish to take both maternity leave and maternity absence. I understand that I have completed a sufficient period of continuous employment with you to be entitled to maternity absence. I enclose a medical/maternity certificate date _____ from Dr. _____.

The expected week of childbirth is _____ and I intend to start taking my maternity leave on _____. I understand that I am entitled to 18 weeks' maternity leave, and thereafter maternity absence until the end of the 29th week after the week in which I give birth. I intend to exercise the right to return to work after that date.

I wish also to receive the Statutory Maternity Pay to which I am entitled during my maternity leave.

Yours sincerely,

_____

MATERNITY LEAVE EMPLOYEE INTENDING TO TAKE MATERNITY ABSENCE: LETTER FROM EMPLOYER

Date _____

To _____

_____

_____

Dear _____

It is now _____ weeks since the birth of your baby, and I hope all is going well. The purpose of this letter is to find out whether you will be returning to work after your maternity absence as planned.

Please write and let me know of your intentions regarding returning to work and the date on which you expect to return, if that is the case.

As a reminder, to preserve your right to return to your old job, you must write to me within 14 days of receipt of this letter and not less than 21 days before you expect to return, confirming your intention and the expected date of return.

Yours sincerely,

_____

MATERNITY LEAVE REQUEST TO EMPLOYER

Date _____

To _____

_____

_____

Dear _____

This is to inform you that I am pregnant and wish to take maternity leave. I enclose a medical/ maternity certificate dated_____ from Dr _____.

The expected week of childbirth is _____ and I intend to start taking my maternity leave on _____. I understand that I am entitled to 18 weeks' leave in total by law.

Please also let me know if I am entitled to receive Statutory Maternity Pay during my maternity leave.

Your sincerely,

_____

SYMPATHY LETTER 1

Date _____

To _____

_____

_____

Dear _____

I was very sorry to hear about the accident that has resulted in your admission into hospital. My sympathies are with you.

Your duties have been assigned to your co-workers, and needless to say, you are missed.

We will all be very happy to see you back at your desk when you are well and ready to return.

Yours sincerely,

_____

SYMPATHY LETTER 2

Date _____

To _____

_____

_____

Dear _____

I was terribly sorry to learn you are in the hospital. I understand it is not too serious and you will be back home soon.

Please accept my best wishes for a speedy recovery. I hope you are back at your desk in the shortest time possible.

You are very much in the thoughts of all of us here, and we all hope to see you soon.

Yours sincerely,

_____

SYMPATHY LETTER 3

Date _____

To _____

_____

_____

Dear _____

I just heard about your accident, and I hope you will have started to feel better by the time this letter reaches you.

Everyone here is thinking of you, and sends their wishes for your speedy recovery.

In the meantime, please call if there is anything we can do for either you or your family.

Yours sincerely,

_____

SYMPATHY LETTER 4

Date _____

To _____

_____

_____

Dear _____

_____ me this morning that you are ill. I hope you will be feeling better by the time this reaches you.

Everyone at the office misses you, but we hope you will take your time coming back and be sure your recovery is complete.

Best wishes from all of us.

Yours sincerely,

_____

Section 5
Performance Evaluation

Note: this section contains notices and letters concerning employee conduct and discipline. It is important that if a company has a disciplinary procedure in place it should be strictly followed .

Disciplinary Action:

Disciplinary Notice – Notice to employee of consequences faced if performance isn't improved.

Disciplinary Report – Records disciplinary action taken for an employee's poor performance.

Disciplinary Warning – Warns employee of company's next action if performance isn't improved.

Excessive Absenteeism Warning – Warns employee of excessive absenteeism.

Final Warning Before Dismissal – Last disciplinary warning to an employee before dismissal.

Final Warning for Lateness – Last warning to employee regarding tardiness before dismissal.

First Warning for Lateness – First written warning to employee regarding tardiness.

First Warning Notice – First notice to employee regarding need to improve performance.

Incident Report – Records information about an incident requiring disciplinary action.

Late Report - Supervisor's report of employee's late arrival.

Probation Notice – Notifies employee of probationary period to improve performance.

Probation Notice: Extended – Notifies employee that probation has been extended.

Second Warning for Lateness – Second warning to employee regarding tardiness.

Second Warning Notice – Second notice to employee regarding need to improve performance.

Suspension Notice – Notifies employee of suspension without pay.

Evaluation:

30-Day Evaluation Notice – Notifies employee of the need to improve performance or face termination.

Coaching Form – Outlines employee's strengths and weaknesses.

Commendation Letter – Letter commending employee on performance.

Consultation of Employee – Records information about a consultation with employee.

Evaluation: Managerial – Supervisor's evaluation of employee as management material.

Evaluation: New Employee – Supervisor's evaluation of new employee's job performance.

Evaluation: Production Personnel – Evaluation of production personnel.

Evaluation: Sales Personnel – Evaluation of sales personnel.

Evaluation: Standard – Standard evaluation form.

Evaluation: Temporary Employee – Evaluation of temporary employee.

Performance Analysis Worksheet – Analyses employee's own job performance.

Performance Appraisal Interview Report – Records results of an employee's performance appraisal interview.

Performance Checklist – Supervisor's list of employee skills and qualities being rated.

Performance Evaluation – Employee job performance evaluation.

Performance Improvement Plan – Outlines employee's action to correct performance.

Performance Objectives – Establishes objectives for performance.

Performance Review – Shows areas employee can improve performance.

Rating Response – Records employee's response to supervisor's evaluation.

Self-Evaluation Form – Employee's evaluation of his/her own job performance.

Grievances:

Complaint Response to Employee – A letter requesting an employee follow a formal complaints procedure.

Counselling Activity Sheet – Records information about a counselling session with employee.

Grievance Form - Records an employee's complaint.

Grievance Investigation Result Notice – Reply to an employee's complaint.

DISCIPLINARY NOTICE

Employee: _____ Department: _____

Written Warning (   )   Final Warning (   )

1. Statement of the problem: (breach of rules, policies, standards or practices, or unsatisfactory performance)

2. Prior, if any, discussion or warnings on this subject, whether oral or written. (list dates):

3. Company policy on this subject:

4. Summary of corrective action to be taken by the company and/or employee:

5. Consequences of failure to improve performance or correct behaviour:

6. Employee statement: (continue on reverse, if necessary)

_____   _____
Employee   Date

_____   _____
Supervisor   Date

DISCIPLINARY REPORT

Employee: _____ Date: _____

Department: _____

Nature of offence: _____

Date of offence: _____ Time: _____

Location of offence: _____

Reported by: _____ Title: _____

Department: _____

Witnesses: _____

Comments: _____

_____

_____

_____

_____

_____   _____
Supervisor   Date

_____   _____
Employee   Date

Offence Number: _____ Date of last offence: _____

Past action taken: _____

Recommendations: _____

_____

The above offence(s) has been documented and made a part of the above employee's personnel file.

_____   _____
Personnel department   Date

DISCIPLINARY WARNING

Employee: _____ Department:_____

Position: _____

Date of Incident:_____ Incident: _____

Reason for Notice: _____

_____

Action taken on this notice:

_____ First warning - verbal

_____ Second warning - written

_____ Suspension for   days

_____ Other (specify): _____

_____

Next step for repeated infraction:

_____ Second warning - written

_____ Suspension for _____ days

_____ Other (specify): _____

_____

Supervisor Comments: _____

_____

Employee Comments: _____

_____

_____   _____
Supervisor   Date

_____   _____
Employee   Date

EXCESSIVE ABSENTEEISM WARNING

Date _____

To _____

_____

_____

Dear _____

In accordance with company policy, this letter is to serve as a written warning for your excessive absenteeism. You must immediately improve your attendance record to acceptable standards or further discipline, including termination, may result.

On several occasions I have spoken to you about your poor attendance record, and improvement was noticed for a time. However, your excessive absences have always resumed. For the period covering _____ to _____, you were absent _____ days, excluding holidays and bank holidays. These absences are detailed below:

Reason: *Days:*

_____   _____

_____   _____

_____   _____

_____   _____

_____   _____

Any unauthorised future absences may result in dismissal.

Yours sincerely,

_____

FINAL WARNING BEFORE DISMISSAL

Date _____

To _____

_____

_____

Dear _____

Further to our meeting, I write to confirm our discussion. You have already been warned about your conduct within this Company. Incidents that have since come to our notice are:

_____

_____

_____

_____

There has not been a satisfactory improvement in your conduct since your last warning. Accordingly, any continued violations of company policy or failure to conduct yourself according to the rules of the company shall result in immediate termination of your employment without further warning.

We remind you that you have the right of appeal against this warning according to the Terms and Conditions of Employment as supplied to you, and if you wish to exercise this right please notify me in writing within _____ working days.

Please contact the undersigned or your supervisor if you have any questions.

Yours sincerely,

_____

FINAL WARNING FOR LATENESS

Date _____

To _____

_____

_____

Dear _____

I refer to our meeting of _____. Despite our verbal and written warnings to you about your time-keeping, there has been no improvement and you have given no satisfactory explanation as to why you continue to be late for work.

Your behaviour is unacceptable. We therefore give you this final warning. If you are late again without offering a reasonable excuse, you will be dismissed.

We remind you that you have the right of appeal against this warning according to the Statement of Terms and Conditions of Employment as supplied to you, and if you wish to exercise this right, please notify me in writing within ____ working days.

Please contact the undersigned or your superior of you have any questions.

Yours sincerely,

_____

FIRST WARNING FOR LATENESS

Date _____

To _____

_____

_____

Dear _____

I refer to our meeting of _____ .You are aware that your hours of work are from _____ a.m. to _____ p.m.. You have repeatedly arrived for work late.

You have been advised of your bad time-keeping and warned of the possible consequences. Despite those warnings you continue to be late for work and have offered no reasonable excuse.

Consider this a formal letter of warning. You must be at your place of work strictly in accordance with the terms of your employment and the hours set. If you are late again without reasonable excuse, disciplinary action will be taken.

This warning is being recorded on your personnel file. You have a right to appeal against this warning, and if you wish to exercise this right, please notify me in writing within _____ working days.

Yours sincerely,

_____

FIRST WARNING NOTICE

Employee: _____ Employee No.: _____

Shift: _____ Date of warning: _____

Date of violation: _____ Time of violation: _____

Violation

_____ Intoxication or drugs   _____ Sub-standard work   _____ Disobedience

_____ Clocking out ahead of time   _____ Wrongful conduct   _____ Tardiness

_____ Clocking out wrong time card _____ Carelessness   _____ Absenteeism

_____ Other: _____

Action Taken: _____

_____

_____

Additional Remarks: _____

_____

_____

Employee Comments: _____

_____

_____

This is your first warning of a company rules violation or of unsatisfactory performance. Future violations may lead to immediate dismissal without further notice.

_____
Employee

_____
Supervisor

_____
Personnel Manager

INCIDENT REPORT

Employee: _____ Date: _____

Department:_____ Supervisor: _____

Date of incident: _____

Describe incident:_____

_____

_____

_____

Action taken: _____

_____

_____

_____

Witnesses:

Name   Address

_____   _____

_____   _____

_____   _____

_____   _____

Reported to:

Person   Date

_____   _____

_____   _____

_____   _____

Use separate sheet for additional remarks.

LATE REPORT

Employee: _____

Date: _____

Department: _____

Time Due at Work: _____ Arrival Time: _____ Time Missed: _____

Did Employee notify Company? Yes ( ) No ( )

Reason for being late: _____

_____

_____

_____

_____

Action Taken:

_____ None

_____ Deduct pay

_____ Make up time

_____ Warning

_____ Dismiss

_____ Other: _____

Comments: _____

_____

_____

_____

_____

_____   _____
Signed   Date

Title: _____

PROBATION NOTICE

Date _____

To _____

_____

_____

Dear _____

You have received _____ earlier written warnings of unsatisfactory performance or violation of our personnel rules.

As you can understand, we do everything possible to retain good employees. When repeated violations or poor performance continues, we usually have no other choice but to dismiss the employee.

However, we do want to give you one final opportunity to prove your value to our company. With that objective we are placing you on a _____-month probationary period. If there is continued unsatisfactory performance during this probationary period, we shall have no alternative but to terminate your employment.

Please accept this as a chance to prove to both yourself and us that our confidence in you is justified.

Please contact _____ upon receipt of this notice, as we do want to review your employment record with you, clarify the conditions of probation and assist you in whatever way possible toward improved performance. Yours sincerely

Yours sincerely,

_____

Copies to:

PROBATION NOTICE: EXTENDED

Date _____

To _____

_____

_____

Dear _____

We refer to our notice of probation dated_____.

We have seen an improvement in your job performance during this probationary period, but the problems identified, as set out in our letter dated _____ have not been entirely eradicated. We believe therefore that it would be in the best interests of both yourself and the company to extend the probationary period so we may better monitor your job performance and make appropriate recommendations for your future employment.

We therefore hereby extend your probation for a period of _____month(s), from _____to_____, and trust you understand our reason for this action.

Once again, we want to continue to work closely with you during this probationary period and help you to improve further your performance and develop as a valued employee. Please contact me so we may arrange a meeting to review your progress.

Yours sincerely,

_____

SECOND WARNING FOR LATENESS

Date _____

To _____

_____

_____

Dear _____

Further to our meeting, I write to confirm the outcome of our discussion about your bad time-keeping, for which you have already been warned.

Despite these verbal and written warnings, you continue to be late for work, in breach of your employment terms. Your hours of work are stated in the Statement of Terms and Conditions of Employment previously given to you. A further copy of the terms and conditions is enclosed.

Since you appear to have ignored the previous warnings, I have no alternative but to issue this second formal warning. If you fail to improve your time-keeping, we may have no option but to consider your dismissal.

This second written warning is being recorded on your personnel file. If you wish to exercise your right of appeal against this warning, please notify me in writing within _____ working days

Yours sincerely,

_____

SECOND WARNING NOTICE

Employee: _____ Employee No.: _____

Shift: _____ Date of warning: _____

Date of violation: _____ Time of violation: _____

Violation

_____ Intoxication or drugs   _____ Substandard work   _____ Disobedience

_____ Clocking out ahead of time   _____ Wrongful conduct   _____ Tardiness

_____ Clocking out wrong time card   _____ Carelessness   _____ Absenteeism

_____ Other: _____

Action Taken: _____

_____

_____

Additional Remarks: _____

_____

_____

Employee Comments: _____

_____

_____

This is your second warning for a breach of company rules or unsatisfactory performance. Future violations may lead to immediate dismissal without further notice.

_____
Employee

_____
Supervisor

_____
Personnel Manager

SUSPENSION NOTICE

Date _____

To _____

_____

_____

You have received informal notices that your conduct has been found to be unsatisfactory. On _____ a formal Warning Notice was placed on your permanent employment record. Your unacceptable conduct has continued; in particular you have:

_____

_____

_____

You are herewith suspended from work for a period of _____ commencing _____. Suspension shall be without pay; however, your health and pension benefits shall continue during the suspension providing you return to work immediately following the suspension period.

YOU MAY BE SUBJECT TO DISMISSAL IN THE FUTURE IF YOU CONTINUE TO VIOLATE COMPANY POLICY.

_____

Company Representative

ACKNOWLEDGED

Date _____

_____

Employee

[**Note:** An employer is only entitled to suspend in this way if the contract allows it to do so, or if its disciplinary policy allows it to do so.]

30-DAY EVALUATION NOTICE

Date _____

To _____

_____

_____

Dear _____

As a result of your failure to correct the problem described below, even after discussions, which included an oral warning, and a written warning dated_____, you are now being placed on a 30-day formal evaluation programme, effective from _____.

As we discussed earlier, the problem with your performance is:

_____

_____

_____

The targets we agreed upon for your period of evaluation are:

_____

_____

_____

I have scheduled a meeting with you on   to consider and discuss with you your progress during this period. I will be available for discussions and guidance at any time during this evaluation programme. I hope this action will result in positive improvement. Failure to correct this situation, however, may result in your dismissal if there is little or no improvement shown at the end of the evaluation period.

Supervisor _____   Date _____

Supervisor's Manager _____   Date _____

Employee _____   Date _____

Personnel Manager _____   Date _____

COACHING FORM

Employee: _____ Date: _____

Department: _____ Supervisor: _____

Reason: _____

Comments:

Weak points are	Strong points are
_____	_____
_____	_____
_____	_____
_____	_____

These weaknesses can be strengthened by:	These strengths can be used more effectively by:
_____	_____
_____	_____
_____	_____
_____	_____
_____	_____
_____	_____
_____	_____
_____	_____

_____   _____
Supervisor   Title

A copy of this report has been given to me and has been discussed with me.

_____   _____
Employee   Date

COMMENDATION LETTER

Date _____

To _____

_____

_____

Dear _____

On behalf of our company, I am very pleased to commend you on your excellent job performance during this last review period from _____ to _____.

Your efforts on behalf of the company are truly appreciated. Only through the devoted and tireless contributions of valued employees like yourself can we confidently look to the future.

Again, on behalf of the company and your co-employees, we salute you for a job well done.

Yours sincerely,

_____

Copies to: Department/Personnel File

CONSULTATION OF EMPLOYEE

Employee: _____ Department: _____

Nature of Problem: _____

Date of Problem: _____

Warning: First (   )   Second (   )   Third (   )

Suspension: From: _____ to _____ Return to Work: _____

Dismissal: _____

Description of Problem: _____

_____

_____

_____

_____

Disciplinary action to be taken: _____

_____

_____

_____

_____

Employee Statement: _____

_____

_____

_____

_____   _____
Supervisor   Date

_____   _____
Employee   Date

EVALUATION: MANAGERIAL

Name: _____ Date: _____

Position/Title: _____ Supervisor: _____

PART I. Performance Assessment

Objectives: _____

_____

_____

_____

_____

_____

Rating: Outstanding( ) Excellent( ) Good( ) Fair( ) Unsatisfactory( )

PART II: Current Potential Assessment

_____ Promotable

_____ Promotable with additional experience/training

_____ Limited or no potential

Reasons for above Evaluation:_____

_____

_____

_____

Employee Career Goals: _____

_____

_____

_____

PART III: Developmental Plans

Major areas requiring performance improvement: _____

_____

continued on next page

_____

_____

_____

Action plan for improvement: _____

_____

_____

_____

_____

Completion Date:_____

Other Comments: _____

_____

_____

_____

_____   _____
Signed/Title   Date

_____   _____
Signed/Title   Date

Evaluation discussed with employee on (date):_____

EVALUATION: NEW EMPLOYEE

Employee: _____ Date: _____

Employment Date:_____ Department: _____

Probation Period: _____ Supervisor: _____

	Excellent	Good	Fair	Poor
Quality of Work:	_____	_____	_____	_____
Quantity of Work:	_____	_____	_____	_____
Knowledge of Job:	_____	_____	_____	_____
Dependability:	_____	_____	_____	_____
Working Relations:	_____	_____	_____	_____
Attitude:	_____	_____	_____	_____
Co-operation:	_____	_____	_____	_____
Potential:	_____	_____	_____	_____

1. This employee should be: Retained (   )   Promoted (   )   Dismissed (   )
    Why? _____
    _____
    _____
    _____
    _____

2. What are employee's weaknesses/deficiencies? What steps should be taken to correct deficiencies?
    _____
    _____
    _____

3. What strengths does this employee have? How can they best be used by company
    _____
    _____
    _____

continued on next page

4. What are this employee's long-term employment prospects?

    _____

    _____

    _____

    _____

5. Is the employee dissatisfied with the company? The position? What steps should be taken to improve working/job conditions?

    _____

    _____

    _____

    _____

6. Other comments on employee's performance, work, record, potential, etc.

    _____

    _____

    _____

    _____

                                        _____
                                        Supervisor

EVALUATION: PRODUCTION PERSONNEL

Employee: _____ Date: _____

Started Work: _____ Review Date:_____

Department:_____ Supervisor: _____

General Performance:	Excellent	Good	Fair	Poor
Attitude:	_____	_____	_____	_____
Skills:	_____	_____	_____	_____
Punctuality:	_____	_____	_____	_____
Dependability:	_____	_____	_____	_____
Initiative:	_____	_____	_____	_____
Co-operation:	_____	_____	_____	_____
Productivity:	_____	_____	_____	_____
Work Quality:	_____	_____	_____	_____

Comments:_____

_____

_____

_____

_____

_____

_____

Comparison to Last Rating: _____

_____

_____

_____

Supervisor

EVALUATION: SALES PERSONNEL

Employee: _____ Date: _____

Territory: _____

Period from:_____ to _____

Sales Performance:

                    Net Sales   _____

               Sales Target   _____

     Above/Below Target By   _____%

Sales Activity:

         Sales Calls/Week   _____

Sales Reports:

        Quality of Reports   _____

     Timeliness of Reports   _____

Other Comments: _____

_____

_____

_____

_____

                                 _____

                                 Signed/Title

EVALUATION: STANDARD

Employee: _____ Date: _____

Department: _____ Supervisor: _____

Period from: _____ to_____

Knowledge of Job: _____

_____

_____

_____

_____

Quality of Work: _____

_____

_____

_____

_____

Productivity: _____

_____

_____

_____

_____

Dependability: _____

_____

_____

_____

_____

Co-operation: _____

_____

_____

_____

_____

continued on next page

Attitude: _____

_____

_____

_____

Punctuality: _____

_____

_____

_____

Overall Rating: _____

_____

_____

_____

_____

_____

Supervisor/Reviewer

_____

Employee

EVALUATION: TEMPORARY EMPLOYEE

Employee: _____ Date Hired: _____

Position: _____

Department: _____ Supervisor: _____

	Excellent	Good	Fair	Poor
Work Quality:	_____	_____	_____	_____
Work Quantity:	_____	_____	_____	_____
Co-operation:	_____	_____	_____	_____
Adaptability:	_____	_____	_____	_____
Initiative:	_____	_____	_____	_____
Dependability:	_____	_____	_____	_____
Appearance:	_____	_____	_____	_____
Attendance:	_____	_____	_____	_____
Punctuality:	_____	_____	_____	_____
Growth Potential:	_____	_____	_____	_____

Recommendations

_____ Permanent hiring as _____ at salary of £ _____

_____ Termination.

_____ Continuation on probationary or temporary status.

_____   _____
Evaluator   Date

PERFORMANCE ANALYSIS WORKSHEET

To (Employee):

To prepare for your upcoming performance review on _____, I would like you to think about the questions that follow, so we can fully utilise the time we have for discussion during your review.

1. How successful overall were you in meeting your performance objectives for this appraisal period?

2. Do you feel your performance objectives are appropriate for your job?

3. Are there areas of concern in your job that you would like to discuss?

4. What strengths do you have that enhance your job performance?

5. What weaknesses do you have that diminish your performance?

6. What additional training do you feel you need in order to do a better job?

7. In what ways can we help you do your job better? Do you feel my supervisory style enables you to or prohibits you from reaching your potential? Why?

8. What are your short-term employment goals? How do you feel you can best achieve these goals?

9. What are your long-range employment goals? How do you feel you can best achieve these goals?

10. What else concerning your job would you like to discuss?

PERFORMANCE APPRAISAL INTERVIEW REPORT

Employee: _____ Date: _____

Department: _____

Reviewed By: _____ Review Period: _____

Objective: _____

Performance Standard: _____

Results: _____

Remarks: _____

Objective: _____

Performance Standard: _____

Results: _____

Remarks: _____

Objective: _____

Performance Standard: _____

Results: _____

Remarks: _____

Supervisor's recommendations: _____

_____

_____

_____   _____

Supervisor   Date

_____   _____

Employee   Date

PERFORMANCE CHECKLIST

Employee: _____ Date: _____

Department: _____ Period from: _____ to _____

Supervisor: _____

	Excellent	Good	Fair	Poor
Honesty:	_____	_____	_____	_____
Productivity:	_____	_____	_____	_____
Quality of Work:	_____	_____	_____	_____
Consistency of work:	_____	_____	_____	_____
Skills:	_____	_____	_____	_____
Enthusiasm:	_____	_____	_____	_____
Attitude:	_____	_____	_____	_____
Co-operation:	_____	_____	_____	_____
Initiative:	_____	_____	_____	_____
Working Relations:	_____	_____	_____	_____
Attendance:	_____	_____	_____	_____
Punctuality:	_____	_____	_____	_____
Dependability:	_____	_____	_____	_____
Appearance:	_____	_____	_____	_____
Other_____:	_____	_____	_____	_____
_____:	_____	_____	_____	_____
_____:	_____	_____	_____	_____

Comments: _____
_____
_____

_____   _____
Supervisor   Date

PERFORMANCE EVALUATION

Employee: _____ Position: _____

Department: _____From: _____ to_____

	Excellent	Good	Fair	Poor
Job Knowledge:	_____	_____	_____	_____
Relations:	_____	_____	_____	_____
Work Quality:	_____	_____	_____	_____
Responsibility:	_____	_____	_____	_____
Quantity of work:	_____	_____	_____	_____
Enthusiasm:	_____	_____	_____	_____
Attitude:	_____	_____	_____	_____
Initiative:	_____	_____	_____	_____
Attendance:	_____	_____	_____	_____
Appearance:	_____	_____	_____	_____
Dependability:	_____	_____	_____	_____
Overall rating:	_____	_____	_____	_____

For Probationary Rating Only:

Recommended for: Permanent Employment (   )   Dismissal (   )

_____
Signed

PERFORMANCE IMPROVEMENT PLAN

Employee: _____ Position: _____

Department: _____ Supervisor: _____

Performance Review Date: _____

Overall Performance Rating: _____

Areas of deficiency: _____

_____

_____

Reasons contributing to poor performance: _____

_____

_____

Corrective action to be taken by employee: _____

_____

_____

Assistance provided by supervisor: _____

_____

_____

Next performance review scheduled: _____

Comments: _____

_____

_____

_____

_____

_____   _____
Employee   Date

_____   _____
Supervisor   Date

PERFORMANCE OBJECTIVES

Employee: _____ Date: _____

Performance Objectives

1. _____

   _____

2. _____

   _____

3. _____

   _____

4. _____

   _____

5. _____

   _____

6. _____

   _____

Presented to and reviewed with employee.

_____   _____

Employee   Date

_____   _____

Supervisor   Date

PERFORMANCE REVIEW

Employee: _____ Date: _____

Position: _____ Date Hired: _____

Department: _____ Supervisor:_____

Appraisal Period From: _____ to _____

Merit ( )   Transfer ( )   Promotion ( )   Other ( )_____

List employee's strengths.

_____

_____

_____

_____

_____

_____

Provide specific examples of employee's major achievements during the review period.

_____

_____

_____

_____

_____

_____

_____

_____

How can employee improve performance?

_____

_____

_____

_____

_____

_____

RATING RESPONSE

Employee: _____

Performance Evaluation Dated: _____

1.   I have discussed with my supervisor the evaluation of my past performance. I ____ agree ____ do not agree with ____all ____some of the conclusions reached, because:

_____

_____

_____

2.   I feel that my performance review ____was ____was not fair and impartial, because:

_____

_____

_____

3.   If I could make changes or improvements in my work or company policies, I would suggest:

_____

_____

_____

_____   _____
Supervisor   Date

_____   _____
Employee   Date

_____   _____
Evaluator   Date

SELF-EVALUATION FORM

CONFIDENTIAL

Employee: _____ Date: _____

My most successful job accomplishments since last performance period are:

1. _____
2. _____
3. _____
4. _____

My least successful job accomplishments since last performance period are:

1. _____
2. _____
3. _____

My key strengths are:

1. _____
2. _____
3. _____

My weakest areas are:

1. _____
2. _____

Action I will take to improve performance: _____

_____

_____

_____

COMPLAINT RESPONSE TO EMPLOYEE

Date _____

Ref _____

To _____

_____

_____

Dear _____

We acknowledge receipt of your letter dated _____ regarding your complaint about:

_____

_____

_____

_____

As you are aware, the company follows a standard complaints procedure in these circumstances. I would be grateful if you could complete the attached form and return it to the Personnel Manager as quickly as possible so that we may follow that procedure. An investigation will then be made into the matter.

Yours sincerely,

_____

COUNSELLING ACTIVITY SHEET

Employee: _____ Date: _____

Time in: _____ Time out: _____

Employee relations staff member: _____

Please tick one of the following:

_____ Career planning

_____ Compensation/Benefits

_____ Job posting

_____ Disciplinary problems

_____ Other: _____

Briefly state the problem: _____

_____

_____

_____

Necessary follow-up sessions:

_____

_____

_____

Results/Solution or outcome of session(s): _____

_____

_____

_____

_____
Supervisor

GRIEVANCE FORM

Employee: _____ Date: _____

Department: _____

State your grievance in detail, with date(s):

_____

_____

_____

Identify other employees with personal knowledge or experience of your grievance:

_____

_____

_____

State briefly your efforts to resolve this grievance:_____

_____

_____

_____

Describe the remedy or solution you seek: _____

_____

_____

_____

_____   _____

Employee   Date

GRIEVANCE INVESTIGATION RESULT NOTICE

Date _____

Ref _____

To _____

_____

_____

Dear _____

I am writing to let you know that your grievance relating to_____
_____has been fully investigated
in accordance with the company's grievance procedures.

Having considered your complaint and having heard all that has been said by you, or on your
behalf, and having taken full account of all that has been said by your trade union representative,
it has been decided_____

_____

_____

_____

This matter has now been fully investigated and whilst I can understand that you may still feel
aggrieved, I am sorry that the matter must now be considered closed.

Yours sincerely,

_____

Section 6
Termination of Employment

Dismissal:

Compromise Agreement: Unfair Dismissal – An agreement between employer and employee to settle a dispute over unfair dismissal.

Dismissal Letter: Capability - Letter to an employee setting out the grounds for dismissal based upon the employee's sub-standard performance.

Dismissal Letter: Intoxication on the Job – Notifies employee of termination because of intoxication on the job.

Dismissal Letter: Sickness - Letter to an employee setting out the grounds for dismissal based upon the employee's poor health.

Instant Dismissal Reasons – A letter to an employee explaining the reasons for instant dismissal.

Termination Checklist – Lists information to be completed upon termination.

Termination of Employment Notice – A letter to an employee giving notice of his termination suitable for an uncontroversial termination, such as for redundancy.

Miscellaneous:

Confidentiality Agreement Notice – Notifies former employee's current employer of employee's confidentiality agreement.

Departure Record – Provides record of items to be returned and completed by terminated employee.

Exit Interview – Employee questionnaire regarding termination, for use only where employee has decided to leave voluntarily.

General Release – Releases employee and company from any liability resulting from employee's employment with company.

Letter to Former Employee who is Using Confidential Information – A letter to a former employee threatening legal action unless use of confidential information ceases.

Mutual Release – Mutually releases employee and company from any liability resulting from employee's employment with company.

Reference Refusal – Refuses to supply requested information on a former employee.

Reference Report – Responds to request for reference on a former employee.

Reference Response – Briefly responds to request for reference on a former employee.

Resignation – Employee's letter of resignation.

Retirement Checklist – Lists information required for retirement.

Redundancy:

Business Transfer Notification – No Redundancy – Notice that employment continues although company has a new owner.

Compromise Agreement: Redundancy – An agreement between employer and employee to settle a dispute over redundancy.

Offer of Employment to Avoid Redundancy – A letter offering alternative employment instead of redundancy.

Redundancy Letter – A letter to an employee giving notice of dismissal by way of redundancy.

Redundancy Notice – A letter notifying an employee of his redundancy and redundancy pay.

COMPROMISE AGREEMENT: UNFAIR DISMISSAL

Date _____

To _____

_____

_____

Dear _____

I hereby confirm the terms we have agreed in relation to the termination of your employment with _____ ("the Company") with effect from _____

1.   The Company will pay you without admission of any liability whatsoever the sum of £2,000 payable immediately on your return of the enclosed copy of this letter as compensation in respect of the claims referred to in paragraph 2 of this letter.

2.   You assert that you may have claims (and therefore could bring proceedings) against the Company for any of the following claims. However, you agree to refrain from initiating any proceedings before an Employment Tribunal alleging that the Company dismissed you unfairly, discriminated against you on the grounds of [race], [sex] or [disability] [or has made an unlawful deduction from your wages] and to withdraw any such proceedings now in progress.

3.   You accept that this payment made by the Company is in full and final settlement of all claims of any kind which you are or might be entitled to make against the Company, its officers, shareholders or employees in connection with your employment or its termination, including any claims which are now proceeding before an Industrial Tribunal.

4.   You will return all property in your possession belonging to the Company on or before _____.

5.   You agree to pay any tax due in respect of the sums referred to above or to reimburse the Company for any tax the Company is required to pay in respect of such sums.

6.   You agree to keep the terms of this agreement confidential

7.   We hereby state that subject to the Solicitors' Indemnity Fund being a 'policy of insurance' for this purpose the conditions regulating this agreement contained in the Employment Rights Act 1996 are satisfied. You, in turn, acknowledge and understand that you are required to take independent legal advice from a qualified lawyer on the terms and effect of this agreement.

continued on next page

Please signify your acceptance of the above by signing and returning the acknowledgement on the enclosed copy of this letter.

Yours sincerely,

_____

Personnel Manager

COMPROMISE AGREEMENT: UNFAIR DISMISSAL ACKNOWLEDGEMENT

I acknowledge receipt of the letter of which the above is a copy and of the sum of £_____

I confirm that I have taken independent advice from _____ solicitors of _____ and I confirm and agree to the terms set out in the letter.

_____   _____
Signed   Date

DISMISSAL LETTER: CAPABILITY

Date _____

To _____

_____

_____

Dear _____

I refer to our meeting on _____.

As I explained at the meeting, you have been unable to carry out your duties to the standards required by the Company. Therefore, we have no alternative but to terminate your employment with the Company with effect from _____.

As you are aware, we have provided you with training and assistance to enable you to improve your performance but without success. In addition, we have attempted to find suitable alternative employment within the Company, but regret that nothing is available.

You are entitled to be paid in full, including any accrued holiday pay, during your notice period.

I take this opportunity of reminding you that you are entitled to appeal against this decision through the Company's disciplinary procedure. If you wish to exercise this right you must let me know within two working days of receipt of this letter.

It is with regret that we have had to take this action. We should like to thank you for your past efforts for the Company and wish you every success for the future.

Yours sincerely,

_____

Personnel Manager

DISMISSAL LETTER: INTOXICATION ON THE JOB

Date _____

To _____

_____

_____

Dear _____

This letter is to inform you that we are terminating your employment with immediate effect from _____. This decision is based on an incident reported to me on _____ by your supervisor, _____. The report recommended your dismissal because of your repeated intoxication during working hours.

As you are aware, the first reported incident of your intoxication on the job was on _____. That report was placed on your personnel file, and you were informed at that time that another incident would result in a disciplinary action or possible dismissal.

This second incident of intoxication adversely affected the operational efficiency and effectiveness of your department and threatened the safety of other employees and this amounts to an act of gross misconduct.

Your final pay cheque, including all forms of compensation due to you, can be picked up in the personnel office on your way out.

Yours sincerely,

_____
Personnel Manager

DISMISSAL LETTER: SICKNESS

Date _____

To _____

_____

_____

Dear _____

I refer to our meeting at your home on _____.

I was very sorry to hear that your condition has not improved and that it is unlikely that you will be able to resume working.

As we discussed, there is little we can do to assist your return to work and our medical adviser has reported that you are not likely to be well enough to return to to your current job for some time, if at all. We have tried to find some alternative suitable work for you but, as you know, all of the work in this Company is fairly heavy work and there is nothing we can offer you.

I regret that I have no alternative other than to give you notice to terminate your employment with the Company with effect from _____.

You are entitled to full pay for the period of your notice plus accrued holiday pay. I shall arrange for these sums to be paid to you, and for your P45 to be sent to you as soon as possible.

If your health does improve in the future to enable you to resume working, I would be pleased to discuss re-employing you.

Yours sincerely,

_____

Personnel Manager

INSTANT DISMISSAL REASONS

Date _____

To _____

_____

_____

Dear _____

Further to the disciplinary hearing held on _____ , I write to confirm, formally, your instant dismissal effective today for the following reason(s):

_____

_____

_____

_____

_____

_____

_____

You are aware of the code of discipline (a copy of which is enclosed) which makes it quite clear that this type of behaviour will result in immediate dismissal. You have the right to appeal against the decision to dismiss you, and if you wish to exercise this right, please notify me of this fact in writing within _____ working days.

Yours sincerely,

_____

ALSO NOTE CONTRACT EMPLOYMENT CLAUSE
'confidentiality'

TERMINATION CHECKLIST

Employee: _____ Date: _____

Department: _____

        _____   Voluntary

        _____   Involuntary

        _____   With Notice

        _____   Without Notice

Reason _____

_____

_____

        _____ Eligible for alternative employment or re-employment?

        _____ Holiday pay period?

        _____ Compromise or Severance Agreement signed?

        _____ Return of all company property, including car, mobile phone, lap-top computer, keys and parking pass, telephone codes, credit cards, personnel manual.

        _____ Pay cheque to employee upon termination

                                           _____

                                           Supervisor

                                           _____

                                           Date

TERMINATION OF EMPLOYMENT NOTICE

Date _____

Ref _____

To _____

_____

_____

Dear _____

In accordance with your contract of employment with us we hereby give you notice of the termination of your employment with us on the _____ day of _____ year _____. The reasons for this decision are:

_____

_____

_____

_____

I regret that this must be written in such formal terms and I want you to know that I deeply regret having to ask that you leave. You understand the circumstances which have brought this about, and I hope that you will soon find other employment to your satisfaction.

Please contact me to discuss further the details of your departure.

Yours sincerely,

_____

CONFIDENTIALITY AGREEMENT NOTICE

Date _____

To _____

_____

_____

Dear _____

It has come to our attention that the above-named individual, whom we previously employed, is now employed by your organisation.

We wish to notify you of certain continuing obligations that_____ has to our company concerning confidential trade secrets and other proprietary information that may have been acquired or developed during this individual's employ with our company.

It is not our intention to prevent this individual, nor any other former employee, from using the general knowledge of the industry or skills acquired while employed by our company. Protecting our company's confidential information is our only concern. As a business organisation also possessing confidential data and trade secrets, you can appreciate our position, I am sure. Your co-operation in this matter will be greatly appreciated.

For information purposes, I am also sending a copy of this letter to:

_____

Yours sincerely,

_____
Personnel Manager

DEPARTURE RECORD

Employee: _____ Department: _____

Termination Date: _____

Complete or return each of the below ticked items upon termination.

Return	(tick)	(tick)	Complete	(tick)	(tick)
ID Badge:	_____	_____	Exit Interview	_____	_____
Company Tools:	_____	_____	Expense Reports	_____	_____
Desk/File Keys:	_____	_____	Terminations Form	_____	_____
Mobile phone:	_____	_____	Confidentiality Report	_____	_____
Credit Cards:	_____	_____	Other: _____	_____	_____
Petty Cash Advances:	_____	_____	_____	_____	_____
Expense Accounts:	_____	_____	_____	_____	_____
Keys to Premises:	_____	_____	_____	_____	_____
Catalogue/Sales Items:	_____	_____			
Sample Products:	_____	_____			
Vehicles:	_____	_____			
Company Documents:	_____	_____			
Customer Lists:	_____	_____			
Lap-top computer:	_____	_____			
Other:					
_____	_____	_____			
_____	_____	_____			
_____	_____	_____			

_____   _____

Supervisor   Date

EXIT INTERVIEW

(**Note:** for use only when employee has decided to leave voluntarily)

Employee: _____ Position: _____

Department: _____ Supervisor:_____

Employed From: _____ To:_____

Reason for Employee's giving notice_____

Employee Returned:

____ car	____ mobile phone	____ lap-top computer
____ keys	____ safety equipment	____ tools
____ ID card	____ company documents	____ uniform
____ credit card	____ other company property	____ company vehicle

Employee was informed about restrictions on:

____ trade secrets	____ removing company documents
____ patents	____ employment with competitor (if applicable)

other_____

Employee exit questions/answers:

1. Did management adequately recognise your contributions? _____
_____

2. Did you feel that you had the support of management?_____
_____

3. Were you properly trained for your job?_____
_____

4. Was your work rewarding? _____
_____

5. Were you fairly treated by the company? _____
_____

6. Was your salary adequate? _____
_____

continued on next page

7. How were your working conditions? _____

_____

8. Were you supervised properly? _____

_____

9. Did you understand all company policies? _____

_____

10. Have you seen theft of company property?_____

_____

11. How can the company improve security? _____

_____

12. How can the company improve working conditions?_____

_____

13. What do you feel are the company's strengths?_____

_____

14. What do you feel are the company's weaknesses? _____

_____

15. Other employee comments or suggestions:_____

_____

GENERAL RELEASE

THIS DEED IS MADE the _____ day of _____ year _____

BETWEEN

(1) _____ (the "First Party");and

(2) _____ (the "Second Party").

NOW IT IS HEREBY AGREED as follows:

1.   The First Party forever releases, discharges, acquits and forgives the Second Party from any and all claims, actions, suits, demands, agreements, liabilities, judgment, and proceedings arising from the beginning of time to the date of these presents and as more particularly related to or arising from:

_____

_____

_____

_____

2.   This release shall be binding upon and inure to the benefit of the parties, their successors and assigns.

IN WITNESS OF WHICH the parties have executed this deed the date and year first above written

_____   Signed for and on behalf of the Company
Signed by the Employee

_____   _____
in the presence of (witness)   Director

Name _____

Address _____   _____
                                                                  Director/Secretary

_____

Occupation

LETTER TO FORMER EMPLOYEE WHO IS USING CONFIDENTIAL INFORMATION

Date _____

To _____
_____
_____

Dear _____

It has come to our attention that you are informing our customers that you can supply them at prices below our current price list. You are clearly using the information about our customers and prices that you gained whilst working for us which is a breach of your duty of confidentiality.

Unless you return to us within seven days all customer and price lists that you have in your possession and give us your written promise not to make further use of your knowledge of our customers and business, our solicitors will be instructed to make an immediate application to the courts for an injunction to prevent you approaching our customers, and they will be instructed also to bring proceedings to claim damages from you.

Yours sincerely,

_____

MUTUAL RELEASES

THIS AGREEMENT IS MADE the _____ day of _____ year ____

BETWEEN:

(1) _____ of _____ (the "First Party"); and

(2) _____ of _____ (the "Second Party").

NOW IT IS HEREBY AGREED as follows:

1.   The First Party and the Second Party do hereby completely, mutually and reciprocally release, discharge, acquit and forgive each other from all claims, contracts, actions, demands, agreements, liabilities, and proceedings of every nature and description that either party has or may have against the other, arising from the beginning of time to the date of these presents, including but not necessarily limited to an incident or claim described as:

_____

_____

_____

2.   This release shall be binding upon and inure to the benefit of the parties, their successors and assigns.

IN WITNESS OF WHICH the parties have signed this agreement the day and year first above written

_____   _____
Signed by or on behalf of the First Party   Signed by or on behalf of the Second Party

_____   _____
in the presence of (witness)   in the presence of (witness)

Name _____   Name _____

Address _____   Address _____

_____   _____
Occupation   Occupation

REFERENCE REFUSAL

Date _____

To _____

_____

_____

Dear _____

We have received your request for an employment reference on the above named individual, who was previously employed by us.

While we would like to help you evaluate prospective employees, we regret that we cannot provide you with the requested information. It is our policy to limit information to the dates of employment, which we have completed below.

Yours sincerely,

_____

Personnel Manager

We hope you understand the reasons for our policy.

This confirms the above individual was employed by our company in the position of

_____ between the dates of _____,

and _____.

REFERENCE REPORT

Date _____

To _____

Re _____

Dear _____

In reply to your request for a reference on the above-named former employee, I provide the following information:

1. Position held: _____

2. Dates employed:_____ to _____

3. Salary on termination: _____

4. Reason for termination: _____

_____

5. Overall performance: _____

_____

_____

6. Other comments: _____

_____

_____

We request that you keep this reference confidential.

Yours sincerely,

_____
Personnel Manager

REFERENCE RESPONSE

Employee:_____

Dates of service: From_____ to_____

Position at dismissal:_____

Reason for dismissal:_____

Note: This company has a policy of issuing brief, standardised reports in response to all employment reference requests. This report is used for all employees. The lack of any further information should not be interpreted as either a favourable or unfavourable reference.

Submitted by: _____   Title:_____

Company: _____   Date: _____

RESIGNATION

Date _____

Ref _____

To _____

_____

_____

Dear _____

This is to inform you that I hereby tender my resignation from the Company with effect from _____. Please acknowledge receipt and acceptance of this resignation by signing below and returning to me a copy of this letter.

Yours sincerely,

Name _____

Address _____

_____

_____

The foregoing resignation is hereby accepted and is effective from the _____ day of _____ _____ year _____.

Name _____

Company _____

[Note: Resignation without giving the required contractual or statutory minimum notice may have legal consequences.]

RETIREMENT CHECKLIST

Employee: _____ Department: _____

1. Letter of Retirement- Submit a Retirement Letter reminding the company of your upcoming retirement to your supervisor who will forward it to the Human Resources Department. Please include your forwarding address in your letter.

2. Holiday Pay - All holiday earned but not taken prior to retirement will be included in your final pay.

3. Address Change - Your address will be changed automatically when you retire and you will receive your statements at home.

4. Employee Benefits - Contact the Employee Benefits Department for information concerning your pension and any other benefit coverage.

5. Company Property - If you have been issued any of the following, please arrange to return them to your supervisor:

_____ Company car   _____ Mobile phone

_____ Security badge   _____ Supervisor's manual

_____ Lap-top computer   _____ Keys

_____ Other _____

BUSINESS TRANSFER NOTIFICATION

Date _____

Ref _____

To Trade Union Representative/Employee Representative

_____

_____

Dear _____

I am writing to you in accordance with Regulation 10 of the Transfer of Undertakings (Protection of Employment) Regulations 1981 ('the Regulations') to inform you of a proposal to transfer the business of _____.

It is proposed that the transfer of the Company will take place on or about _____. The reason for the transfer is that _____.

The proposed transfer will affect the following employees _____. From a legal standpoint, the affected employees will, by virtue of the operation of the Regulations, transfer on their existing terms and conditions of employment and with continuity of employment for statutory and contractual purposes. [State whether there will be any social or economic implications of the transfer - economic would include loss of pension rights.]

It [is][is not] envisaged that the Company or [name of Transferee] will be taking [any] measures in connection with the transfer in relation to those employees who will be affected by the transfer. [If measures are envisaged state these - if this is the case there is a duty to consult]

Yours sincerely,

_____

COMPROMISE AGREEMENT: REDUNDANCY

Date _____

To _____

_____

_____

Dear _____

It is with regret that I write to inform you that the Company has decided to make you redundant with effect from _____. You are aware of and we have discussed the reasons for your redundancy. We have tried to find you a suitable position commensurate with your abilities elsewhere within the Company but there is nothing available.

The Company has however decided to make you an ex gratia payment of £_____ as compensation for the termination of your employment. In addition, the Company will make you a statutory redundancy payment of £_____.

The statutory redundancy payment is calculated in accordance with your age, salary (subject to a statutory maximum of £_____ per week) and the number of years service with the Company.

1. The Company will therefore pay you a total sum of £_____ payable immediately on your return of the enclosed copy of this letter.

2. You agree to refrain from initiating any proceedings before an Industrial Tribunal alleging that the Company has dismissed you unfairly, discriminated against you on the grounds of race, sex or disability or has made an unlawful deduction from your wages, and to withdraw any such proceedings now in progress.

3. You accept that this payment made by the Company is in full and final settlement of all claims of any kind which you are or might be entitled to make against the Company, its officers, shareholders or employees in connection with your employment or its termination including any claims which are now proceeding before an Industrial Tribunal.

4. You will return all property in your possession belonging to the Company on or before _____.

5. You agree to pay any tax due in respect of the sums referred to above or to reimburse the Company for any tax the Company is required to pay in respect of such sums.

continued on next page

6.   You agree to keep the terms of this agreement confidential.

7.   We hereby state that, subject to the Solicitors' Indemnity Fund being a 'policy of insurance' for this purpose, the conditions regulating this agreement contained in the Employment Rights Act 1996 are satisfied. You, in turn, acknowledge and understand that you are required to take independent legal advice from a qualified lawyer on the terms and effect of this agreement.

Please signify your acceptance of the above by signing and returning the acknowledgement on the enclosed copy of this letter.

Yours sincerely,

_____

Personnel Manager

COMPROMISE AGREEMENT (REDUNDANCY) ACKNOWLEDGEMENT

I acknowledge receipt of the letter of which the above is a copy and of the sum of £_____ referred to in it.

I confirm that I have taken independent advice from _____
solicitors of _____ and I confirm and agree to the terms set out in the letter.

_____   _____
Signed   Date

OFFER OF EMPLOYMENT TO AVOID REDUNDANCY

Date _____

Ref _____

To _____

_____

_____

Dear _____

After consultation with our employees and representatives of_____

_____ Union, we

regretfully conclude that we must close the _____ section

of the company. This will mean redundancy for some employees.

However, I am pleased to advise you that _____ can offer you

suitable alternative employment as a _____. The salary

and terms of employment will approximate to what you are currently receiving from us.

Please confirm to me that you accept this employment offer.

Yours sincerely,

_____

REDUNDANCY LETTER

Date _____

To _____

_____

_____

Dear _____

Further to our meeting, it is with deep regret that I must advise you that your employment with us will end on _____ by reason of redundancy. The company has experienced a serious decline in business.

We are following the following selection criteria:

_____

_____.

Wherever possible, we have offered employees other employment, but unfortunately we have been unable to find a suitable alternative position for you. You are entitled to receive a payment based upon the scale laid down by law and a tax-free cheque for the amount due is enclosed together with a statement reflecting how this has been calculated. You are also entitled to _____ [weeks'][months'] notice [which you will be required to work][which you will not be required to work, and subsequently we enclose a cheque in lieu of your notice period].

We hope that you soon find other suitable employment. If you need a reference from us, please submit our name with the confidence that our reference will be a good one.

Yours sincerely,

_____

REDUNDANCY NOTICE

Date _____

To _____

_____

_____

Dear _____

It is with regret that I write to inform you that the Company had decided to make you redundant with effect from today. You are aware that the Company is being restructured and the volume of work has substantially diminished.

We have tried to find you a suitable position commensurate with your abilities elsewhere within the Company but there is nothing available.

You are entitled to _____ notice of termination but we believe it is better for you and all others concerned if you leave immediately. The Company will pay you a sum of £_____ in the form of an ex gratia payment of compensation for the termination of your employment. This sum is calculated as follows:

(a) _____ weeks' gross salary at £_____ per annum   £_____

(b) _____ days accrued holiday   £_____

In addition, the Company will make you a statutory redundancy payment of £_____. This is calculated in accordance with your age, salary (subject to a statutory maximum of £_____ per week) and the number of years service with the Company.

1. The Company will therefore pay you a total sum of £_____ immediately on your signature and return of the enclosed copy of this letter.

2. You accept that this payment made by the Company is in full and final settlement of your claim for compensation and/or damages for the termination of your employment with effect from today.

3. You will return all property in your possession belonging to the Company.

continued on next page

4.   This sum should be tax free but you agree to pay any tax due in respect of the sums referred to above or to reimburse the Company for any tax the Company is required to pay in respect of such sums.

Please acknowledge receipt of this letter by signing and returning the acknowledgement on the enclosed copy of this letter.

Yours sincerely,

_____

Personnel Manager

I acknowledge receipt of the letter of which the above is a copy and of the sum of £_____ referred to in it.

_____

Signed

MORE BOOKS AVAILABLE FROM LAWPACK

The Buy-to-Let Bible

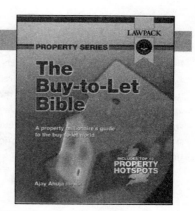

Low mortgage rates and under-performance by traditional savings and investment products means that property has never looked a better way to invest for the future. Author Ajay Ahuja divulges the practical and financial techniques that have made him a millionaire. It covers finding the right property, the right mortgage lender, the right tenant, legal issues and tax. Buy-to-let property 'hotspots' by region across the UK are also listed.

Code B437 | ISBN 1 904053 36 X | Paperback | 245 x 199mm | 136pp | £11.99 | 3rd Edition

Residential Lettings

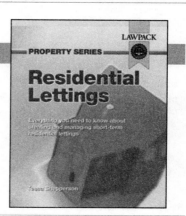

Are you thinking of letting a flat or a house? This guide steers anyone who intends - or already is - letting property through the legal and practical issues involved. It provides all the up-to-date information and tips that a would-be landlord needs. It will also alert existing landlords to the points of good practice that make a letting successful, and the legal obligations that they may not be aware of. For lettings in England & Wales and Scotland.

Code B422 | ISBN 1 904053 63 7 | Paperback | 245 x 199mm | 112pp | £11.99 | 4th edition

House Buying, Selling and Conveyancing

It isn't true that only those who have gone through long, expensive and involved training can possibly understand the intricacies of house buying, selling and conveyancing. This guide is a new, updated edition of a best-selling book by Joseph Bradshaw, once described in The Times as the 'guru of layperson conveyancing', which explains just how straightforward the whole process really is. Required reading for all house buyers (or sellers).

Code B412 | ISBN 1 904053 61 0 | Paperback | 245 x 199mm | 148pp | £11.99 | 4th Edition

To order, visit **www.lawpack.co.uk** or call **020 7394 4040**

MORE BOOKS AVAILABLE FROM LAWPACK

Business Letters I Made Easy

Business Letters I and Business Letters II (see next panel) are complementary Made Easy guides, each providing an invaluable source of more than 100 ready-drafted, annotated letters to take away the headache and time-wasting of letter writing. Business Letters I covers managing suppliers and customers, debt collection, credit control and international trade.

Code B504 | ISBN 1 902646 38 X | Paperback | 250 x 199mm | 160pp | £9.99 | 1st edition

Business Letters II Made Easy

Business Letters II covers employing people, sales and marketing management, banking, insurance and property, business and the community and international trade.

Code B505 | ISBN 1 902646 39 8 | Paperback | 250 x 199mm | 176pp | £9.99 | 1st edition

Employment Law Made Easy

Written by an employment law solicitor, Employment Law Made Easy is a comprehensive, reader-friendly source of reference which will provide answers to practically all your employment law questions. Essential knowledge for employers and employees!

Code B502 | ISBN 1 904053 38 6 | Paperback | 250 x 199mm | 192pp | £9.99 | 4th edition

To order, visit **www.lawpack.co.uk** or call **020 7394 4040**

MORE BOOKS AVAILABLE FROM LAWPACK

Company Minutes & Resolutions Made Easy

Company Minutes & Resolutions Made Easy is what every busy company secretary or record-keeper needs. Maintaining good, up-to-date records is not only sensible business practice, but also a legal requirement of Companies House. This Made Easy guide makes the whole process straightforward. It provides an invaluable source of essential documents that no company should be without.

Code B501 | ISBN 1 902646 41 X | Paperback | 250 x 199mm | 198pp | £9.99 | 1st edition

Debt Collection Made Easy

Chasing debts is a pain which all businesses can do without. Unfortunately, unpaid bills are an all-too frequent problem for business owners and managers. Debt Collection Made Easy helps you solve it. It provides expert advice and tips on resolving disputes, reducing the risks of bad debt, getting money out of reluctant payers, letter cycles, credit insurance, export credit and much more.

Code B512 | ISBN 1 902646 42 8 | Paperback | 250 x 199mm | 144pp | £9.99 | 1st edition

Negotiating Tactics Made Easy

What business can expect success without being able to negotiate good deals? In today's competitive world, you need to know about the tactics and techniques which professional negotiators use to win. Negotiating Tactics Made Easy pools the expertise of 12 experienced negotiators and is packed with advice and tips on handling almost any situation. Be prepared for the ploys and techniques you are bound to come up against!

Code B507 | ISBN 1 902646 45 2 | Paperback | 250 x 199mm | 248pp | £9.99 | 1st edition

To order, visit **www.lawpack.co.uk** or call **020 7394 4040**